T0071680

THE
ARTIST
WITHIN
ME

Other books by John Jacobson

Double Dream Hands

A Place in the Choir

Order from Chaos
(with Cristi Cary Miller)

BOOKS FOR CHILDREN

The Quest
(with Mark Brymer)

A Tree in Tappen Wood
(with Emily Crocker)

www.johnjacobson.com

ISBN-13: 978-1-45842-254-5

Published by Hal Leonard Corporation
7777 W. Bluemound Road
P.O. Box 13819
Milwaukee, WI 53213

Library of Congress Cataloging-in-Publication Data

Jacobson, John.
 The artist within me : a teacher's year of creative discovery / by John Jacobson.
    p. cm.
 ISBN 978-1-4584-2254-5
 1. Jacobson, John. 2. Music teachers–United States–Biography. 3. Music–Instruction and study–United States–Anecdotes. I. Title.
 ML423.J116A3 2012
 780.71–dc23
                            2012034502

THE

ME

A TEACHER'S YEAR
OF CREATIVE DISCOVERY

by
JOHN JACOBSON

Forward

(I mean it!)

I haven't read all of those Chicken Soup for the Soul books. There are a lot of them! But recently a friend sent me a chapter from one that I thought was really good. This particular article challenged the reader to "suppose someone gave you a pen…." It went on to suggest that the pen had only so much ink in it but that you couldn't tell how much. You could write just a little bit and it would run dry or it might last a long time before it ran out. You might get only a few words out or you might create a masterpiece. The poser then challenged the reader to take chances, draw outside the lines, write things that were important to you, plunge ahead with courage and conviction, and so on. Finally he posed another question, "Now, suppose someone gave you a life…."

Hmmm…

I am fortunate to spend much of my life around teachers, specifically teachers of the arts. You are my favorite kind of people. You are selfless, giving, caring, and creative professionals who are among the most qualified at your jobs of anyone on the planet. You make the world more beautiful every single day.

But this selflessness can get you in trouble. Most of you teachers of the arts grew up nurturing your craft and perfecting your talents from a very young age. Then you went on to higher education, where you formalized your training and became experts not only in your chosen art form but in the craft of teaching as well. You were fortunate to be an artist and teacher, a very special combination that not every artist can manage.

As you continued in your teaching, you quickly realized how all-consuming effective teaching could be. Combined with the ever-growing responsibilities that naturally come with adulthood, something had to give. Very often it was your art that was pushed to the side. As the days

1

and years went by, you began to feel that you were no longer much of an artist, or at least that you were not able to give your artistic self the attention you wanted to give it—the attention it deserves.

The world needs you as a teacher and the world needs your contribution as an artist. If *you* don't believe that yet, then at least consider this: You need to contribute as an artist as much as you need to be a teacher of the arts.

And you deserve the chance to practice your art. You've been handed a pen. What are you going to do with it?

With mine, I wrote one page for every day of the year. Even leap day! Three hundred sixty-six ideas. This book won't solve all your problems, make you more creative, or bring to you the perfect life balance we all seem to be searching for. But it might help you begin, day by day, to get back in touch with the artist you still are, the artist that never really left you. It is meant to be a book you pick up and either read right through or read one little page at a time, to give yourself something to do or think about as you reintroduce your teacher self to your artistic self.

In one of his daring compositions, John Cage used the words "Begin anywhere" to instruct the players on how to perform the piece. That's what I suggest you do with this book, with your pen, and with the life that's been handed to you. Perhaps you should read the page that coincides with your birthday and see what I was thinking about that day. Or, start at the end and work backward, or at today's date and go any direction you want to. While some of the pages make more sense if they are read in chronological order, there really is no plot and you're the main character in it. So, "begin anywhere." But do begin.

There is much confusion about who said this first, but Ralph Waldo Emerson or Harold R. McAlindon or maybe Lady Gaga wrote, "Do not go where the path may lead; go instead where there is no path and leave a trail." Jacobson said, "Art can heal the world." And I believe that.

Consider what it is about life that dazzles you. Pick up the pen, the brush, the instrument, the baton—and "begin anywhere," you the teacher and you the artist.

A resolution.

"The best time to plant a tree is twenty years ago.
The second best time is now."
—African proverb

We've all made hundreds of New Year's resolutions that we clearly recognized we would never keep, even as we made them. Well, we can live in regret, or we can try again this year, setting realistic goals and not shying away from them from the get-go.

You are an artist and a teacher. What a remarkable combination. This year's resolution need not be hollow. You've done it before; it's not too late. This year, you will remember and consciously tap into your artistic self, knowing that it will make you a more effective teacher, fulfilled artist, and dynamic human being. Get started. Today.

Connect.

You are not the first person who ever felt that this existence is not what you had in mind for your life, especially your artistic life. (You know what a quarter note is! Why do you have to keep repeating it?) You are not alone, and you don't have to figure it out alone.

The road is well trod: nice to say, perhaps, but daunting in reality. Yet a practical step this early in the year would be to identify others who have gone or are going through what you are going through right now and who may even share in your quest. They may be other teachers in your building, and they most certainly would be other teacher/artists in your community. Make the conscious effort to connect with them, not just to share teaching tips but to explore your feelings and goals as artists who also get to teach.

Find a friend in the mountain.

There is a great story about Sherpa in the Himalayas having a conversation with one of their hiking wards after a day of strenuous hiking. The hikers were incredulous as to how these Sherpa managed to effortlessly move up the mountain, even in its steepest spots and its highest elevations, with hardly a gasp or rapid pulse. The Sherpa responded: "When you look at the mountain, you see it as your enemy, something to be conquered. We see the mountain as our friend that lifts us up and carries us along."

Your artistic/teaching challenge is not your enemy. Your teaching responsibilities are not there to get in your way, nor is your artistic calling a burden to be borne. The things that make up your day-to-day, very human life may seem like mountains blocking your attempt to live fully and in balance. But they are not your enemy. They carry you along. You don't need to conquer them. It's not about winning and losing. It's about recognizing and embracing those challenges as opportunity. It's about living and finding comfort, satisfaction, and inspiration on the climb.

Take a single step.

Wake up to the world you are in. Be receptive to the good around you. It's early in the year, so it's a good time to re-examine your state of affairs. It may not be as bleak as you thought at the end of last semester. We are often blind to the opportunities closest to us.

Think about a realistic step you could take to reawaken the artist that you know is in you. Could you offer to perform for a community event? Could you end a lecture or rehearsal with an artistic expression of your own (a song, a poem, a painting, a ditty)? Do some concrete artistic endeavor. No, not make something out of cement! Try to make an opportunity for an artistic expression of yourself. Do not worry about the quality necessarily. In your mind it will probably not be as good as your senior recital in college—but think how long you worked on that! Just get something started. Not merely on the calendar…but actually start to do it.

Be true to your core and move on.

How many times do we exhort our students to muster the courage to step out of their comfort zones? We encourage them to try something new, even if they think they will not be successful at it; even if they may have tried it before and failed miserably, at least in their own estimation. But at the same time we don't find the courage to do it ourselves?

I believe some things are innate in each of us, by genetic disposition or something close. But I do not believe we are preprogrammed. You can change. Yet in order to do so effectively you have to start by truly examining your very core. What do you really believe about yourself and the world you share with others? Make a list. Not what you have been told. What you believe without having to be told. Now, sincerely look at each of those beliefs and wonder, "With these core beliefs in place, how can I move forward as an artist?" Know that to be an artist you may have to step out of your comfort zone, re-examine your core beliefs, and begin the list again from a new, more mature, and courageous perspective.

Are you brave enough? Of course you are. You stand every day in front of classes full of students who constantly examine your core beliefs for you. Surely you can face them yourself.

⚜

This I believe.

Today's entry is closely related to yesterday's challenge to you to have the courage to re-examine your very core beliefs. I love the "This I Believe" public radio program that engages people from all over the world to write essays describing the core values that guide their daily lives. They've been doing it off and on since the 1950s. Some of the essays are enlightening. All of them are interesting.

I challenge you to take a few minutes, or days if you like, to write your own essay. Start with the sentence "This I believe….." and write what follows. In the public radio series you get 350 to 500 words. But you can write as much as you want. It's your life. They are your beliefs.

If you, as I do, believe that art is a vehicle that helps to illuminate the Truth, perhaps starting with examining what you believe are truths as a human will help as you awaken as an artist.

Concentrate on what you can become.

My friend Tony likes to use a two-word phrase whenever his colleagues are whining or rehashing something bad or inconvenient that happened a long time ago or even yesterday. Tony looks at them and says simply, "It's over!"

He's so right. What happened has happened. What your life was yesterday does not necessarily mean that it is your life forever. The great thing about life is that you get a fresh crack at it every minute of every hour of every day. You're not stuck. You're educated, experienced, talented, and always in a perfect position to try it another way. If you feel the need, let today be that day.

Eat well. Sleep well. Laugh easily.

I once heard of a nunnery in which the only rules for the sisters who lived there were: "Eat well. Sleep well. Laugh easily." I expect the idea was that if all of these three things were in place, so too would be your head, your heart, and your spirit.

I use to tease a friend of mine who happened to be a nun in Hawaii. "Sister," I would say, "I thought that as a nun you were supposed to suffer for the Lord. Good heavens! I could be a nun in Hawaii."

"God doesn't want you or me or anyone else to suffer, John," she replied.

I told her about the "Eat well. Sleep well. Laugh easily" directive I had heard about for another convent.

"Sounds pretty good," she said. "Sounds pretty much like what the good Lord had in mind."

I don't know much about theology. But I'm going with this. Maybe you should too.

⸎⸎⸎

Slop it down.

January 9th might be a little late to be coming up with your New Year's resolutions, but if you're like me, you've probably already broken most of them anyway, so let's start a new list. They can be as broad or as simple as you want them to be. There are no right or wrong answers or ideas. Just slop it down.

I use that "slop it down" phrase because that is what an English professor used to say when we were all struggling to write our term papers: afraid to write the first word, and paralyzed that we might make a mistake, sound silly, or be found out for the intellectual frauds we all knew we were. (Speaking for myself, as a college freshman I quickly learned that everybody on the entire campus and probably in the whole world was smarter, more talented, more confident, and certainly more competent than I. Funny, then, that when I graduated I knew it all.)

This wise professor said: "Slop it down. It doesn't matter what the first draft says, you can always go back and fine-tune or even start all over. But you have to have something to work with."

So this January 9th, write down your craziest, or not-so-crazy, dreams and ambitions and resolutions. No one is going to hold you to them. No one is going to give you a grade. They are just for you. But they'll give you something to work with and you can always fine-tune it or even start all over on January 10th.

Identify what you are enthusiastic about.

If you can stand to look at yesterday's list of dreams and resolutions, spend a moment today identifying on that list the things that you are most enthusiastic about. Hopefully, it's not crawling back in bed until spring. Ask yourself why you are enthusiastic about it. What is it you want?

Conversely, there might be something on your list that you see as an aspiration but that you actually dread.

Make a vow to pursue with vigor that which you are most enthusiastic about. Today, why not do what you love?

Run for. Not against.

I once took a few months off to run for public office. It was a short political noncareer. But I believed it was a good thing to do. I've never really had a bucket list, but if I did, I guess running for office might have been on there. Once I lost, to a really good and honorable opponent, I was never so glad to get back to the comfort zone of my former profession.

One of the stranger questions I was asked by a newspaper reporter during the campaign was "Why do you want to run against this particular incumbent?"

Without thinking, I responded, "I'm not running against anything or anyone at all. I am running for the people I might represent and for the issues that I feel are important to my constituents." Huh? Maybe that's why I didn't win.

I believe you ought to be "for" something. As you examine your artist/teacher self, I encourage you to explore what you are "for" more than what you are against. It will make the journey infinitely more pleasant and, I believe, more productive.

—2/3/9—

Pick up the pace!

I have yet to encounter a sad, tired, or depressed person who walks quickly. Pick up the pace. It's amazing how the energy you spend at this faster tempo will not wear you down but will boost you up.

This is not to say there should be no place (or time) in your life for a quiet amble, but if you feel drained and emotionally spent, you have the tools and you have a choice. Try it. I dare you. It may not solve everything, but it's something you can do all alone to get your creative and emotional juices flowing.

"It's what you do do!"

My dear friend Dr. Tim Lautzenheiser says, "It's not what you can do; it's not what you will do; it's what you do do!"

Seems that both Tim and I got stuck in junior high with our humor, but his observation is anything but juvenile.

How many people do you know who talk a great game about the amazing potential they see in the mirror and the many accomplishments just waiting around the corner? There comes a time when you ought to actually do something with all that talent and potential.

"Just do it." Whatever "it" is on your list. More time for your art? More opportunities for personal and professional development? More time to ponder the sea or the sky? Whatever it is you feel you haven't found the time or energy to do, get yourself in position and do it. No "can." No "will." Just "do do."

Success is nothing to be feared.

Don't be afraid of your success. Yes, it brings more responsibility and higher expectations. But you can handle it.

Move forward.

Take a step in the direction you want to go. Refuse a cookie. Throw away a cigarette; write a word, a verse, a couplet; sign up for a class; take a lesson. Something…

It's fairly unrealistic to think that everything is going to change in one day and that all of the imbalance you sense in your life, real or imaginary, is going to be squared away today. But taking a first small step can be huge. It's sort of like writing this book for me. I knew what I wanted to do, but the idea of writing 366 pieces, even short little ditties such as this, seemed an incredibly daunting task. So one day I just decided to start to try to chip away at it. And lo, I'm already at January 15th!

You chip away, too. Sometimes you might have a spurt where you make tremendous progress toward your goal. Other days, you might feel as though you are getting nowhere. But as long as you are moving, there is progress. Don't worry about how long it's going to take. In the end, it doesn't matter.

I have a friend who signs his letters (yes, he still writes them) "Onward!"

Move "onward!" Good advice.

No sarcasm.

Never be sarcastic with yourself. Don't get me wrong; I love a bit of salty sarcasm as much as the next guy.

"Oh, really? I couldn't tell," I hear you thinking sarcastically.

Okay. You can be sarcastic with me. But don't do it to yourself. Not at this time when you are trying to rediscover the beautiful artist inside you. Comments to yourself like "Yeah, I'm sure this is going to be great!" or "Yeah, right! I'm an artist" with a tsk and a roll of your eyes don't help you or your quest. In truth, they might even be a bit of a copout.

Actually, "this" might truly be great. You might indeed be an "artist" again. But it will be hard for that to happen if you are constantly beating yourself up for your dreams or for what you see as your lack of progress.

I know it sounds a bit hokey, but look in the mirror and say, "This is going to be great." Then go make it so.

In the end your efforts and results may be great only in your own estimation, but there will be progress.

⟞ ⟝

Get out of the warm-up suit.

Take a step out of your comfort zone.

Eleanor Roosevelt said:

> *"You gain strength, courage, and confidence by every experience in which you really stop to look fear in the face. You are able to say to yourself, 'I have lived through this horror. I can take the next thing that comes along.' ... You must do the thing you think you cannot do."*

What is out of your comfort zone is identifiable only by you. But genuine growth happens when you try something new rather than just the same ol' same ol'.

It might be as simple as trying some food you never tried before. In fact, I think that is a pretty good example. I, for one, am often intimidated by delis and sushi bars. There are just too many choices and I never feel comfortable with the lingo. "What's the difference between corned beef and pastrami?" "I'll have a smear of this on challah."

When it comes to sushi, frankly, I still don't know my hamachi from my unagi and I lived in Japan for a year! But, growth happens when you try something new. So today, walk a different path, drive a different route, talk to someone new in the teachers lounge. Go ahead, "look fear in the face" and order the Reuben.

Ask for help.

If I could teach one lesson to every child I ever meet and know that it would stick, I think I would teach them all to remember that they are not alone. There is always someone they can go to for help. There is always someone who cares, who will offer a shoulder to cry on, a piece of advice, or just a pair of ears to hear their thoughts.

As you approach this year of freeing your artistic self, make a list of those people you know you can go to help you figure it out. It might be a professional counselor, a colleague, a minister, a family member, or a friend who will play that role for you. Ask for help. There is no shame in it.

Someday, or perhaps the same day, you will repay the favor with your own set of ears and your own sincere support. Part of the very definition of what it is to be human is that we relate to one another. Be human. Ask for help.

It won't kill you.

So what's the worst that can happen? You try something new that you always wanted to do or you resume doing something that you once loved but gave up for lack of time, energy, support, whatever, and what's going to happen? Are you worried about making a fool of yourself? I always say to teachers, "The kids and most of the rest of the faculty already think the music/art teacher is a little kooky, so you might as well live up to your reputation!"

The fact is, you won't die from writing something lousy or singing off-key or flunking a test. So they think you're kooky—at least they're thinking about you.

Learn some discipline.

Discipline is a learned behavior and has to be practiced. Figure out what it is in your life that you want to change. Refer to the lists you made earlier in the month if you've already forgotten. Do you want to have more free time but haven't learned the art of saying "no"? Do you want to create art as well as teach it? Learn a new skill or have a better relationship with your colleagues, your family, your friends? Do you want to change careers, lose weight, see more of the world, feel more comfortable in your own skin? Like playing the piano or painting a landscape, each of these quests takes practice. You'll get better at it the more you pay attention to it—the more you rehearse.

I once had to fire someone. I dreaded it. She was a very nice person and I considered her a friend. So I practiced on a couple of other friends first. I didn't actually fire them because they didn't work for me, but I did practice how I was going to do this painful chore. Rehearsing helped. When the time came, it wasn't fun, but I was better at it than I would have been had I not practiced. The next time was easier. Now I'm self-employed. I can fire only myself. I like it better.

Angel gear.

On some of the Caribbean Islands, the preferred mode of transportation is a kind of motorized putput that looks like a motorcycle with a bucket in the back for the passengers. They are often wildly decorated, make an awful racket, and may very well be one of the main causes of global warming because of their terrible levels of exhaust emissions. You never really know if they are going to make it up a hill and you really never know if they are going to be able to stop as they careen down the other side. In fact, the islanders use a term called "angel gear," which is basically when you don't worry about gears or brakes and just let 'er fly down the hill, hoping nothing gets in your way because you have no control over stopping or even slowing down. You just leave your fate to the angels.

Sometimes when working at changing the course of your life, it is wise to move slowly, methodically, and in full control of each step. On other occasions, however, it may not be the worst thing in the world to shift it into angel gear, let go the clutch, and let 'er fly. The angels will watch over you and the feeling can be exhilarating. Also, figuratively shifting into angel gear to jump-start your rediscovery of your artistic self is not going to kill you. I'm not so sure about those island putputs.

There are 1.3 billion people in China.

Yes, there will always be someone brighter and faster, who will do "it" more cheaply and perhaps even better than you or I. But that is not a good enough excuse to not make your own worthy contribution to whatever creative cause is at hand. So often we are afraid to express ourselves artistically because we don't feel we will ever be the best, or even very good at it at all. How many times have you come home from a recital or a concert and thought: "I'm never going to sing, dance, or play again." "I'll never be as good as that." "I might as well quit."

It's going to be a pretty frustrating life if you do only the things you are the best in the world at. Creating art is not a contest. It is about expressing yourself. It is about enjoying the process. It is even about relishing the idea that somewhere in the world there is art that might make yours seem rough. Figure out why you want to do your art. Don't worry about China. Today, just worry about yourself.

Nix the neurosis.

Way back in the 1930s, Swiss psychiatrist Carl Jung wrote in his book *Modern Man in Search of a Soul*: "About a third of my cases are suffering from no clinically definable neurosis, but from the senselessness and emptiness of their lives. This can be described as the general neurosis of our time."

Is it any different today? Some people don't seem to have any problem at all. But many people struggle as they try to define the true meaning to their life. Parents might list their children. That seems obvious. Teachers have their students. Artists have their art. If you are a teacher and an artist you have two of those three. You may also be a parent. Three for three. This is a pretty good start to your list of what can fill the "senselessness and emptiness" of your life. Just naming the meaning of your life may not be enough for you. But go ahead, name three more. That ought to get you through until January 24th.

25

The meaning of life.

I suppose if I reveal to you the meaning of life on January 24th there will be little reason to read the rest of this book. Oh well, I think it is worth the risk. I'm going to tell you now.

You might think that nobody is qualified to explain the true meaning of life. But not being qualified has not stopped me yet. So, here is what I think.

If you are interested in finding the meaning of life, find something meaningful to do with your life.

Making art and teaching: two meaningful things to do. There, I said it. Amen.

Take control.

Is it a person or people that stand in the way of your goals and ambitions? If so, we know we can handle that. Now that you have defined what you want, it may be time to approach those people or that person and state your case. Here are five ground rules for engagement.

1. No whining or complaining.
2. Hold your ground.
3. Never act like a victim.
4. Be passionate about your convictions without losing control.
5. Did I say "no whining"?

I think these five rules should apply whether you are defending your department against budget cuts, asking for a lighter load so you can do a better job at all of it, justifying your very existence to those around you—or even when you are alone, looking in the mirror and strategizing your next step in freeing up your artist self.

Prepare yourself.

Perhaps "prepare yourself" should have been another one of the rules of engagement we talked about way back on January 25th. I don't think the importance of being prepared for the steps ahead can be overstated.

How much more fun and effective is it to teach a class that you feel well prepared for? How much more rewarding is it to perform if you have had ample rehearsal time?

So, ask yourself what you can do to prepare yourself for the artistic adventures that lie ahead. Is it to take a new class, join a club, read a book, go to a conference, free up some regular time on the calendar, learn a new skill, or schedule regular practice time—time spent on you and your artistic pursuits?

That's why you went to school, right? To prepare yourself so that when opportunity reared its beautiful head you were ready to succeed. Now, what preparations do you need to make to prepare yourself for your next artistic journey?

Let this moment linger.

Did you know that the German playwright Johann Wolfgang von Goethe spent parts of his entire adult life writing Faust? I don't think that was his plan when he started writing it. I guess he just felt that he could always make it better or that the process of the work's creation was what gave him satisfaction as an artist.

Your work as an artist may never be finished. Hopefully, not. Because you are also a teacher there will be times when you have more opportunity to pursue your own artistic endeavors than at other times. That's the nature of the beast. One essential is to not kick yourself when you feel as if you haven't the time, energy, or inclination to do the artistic work you so badly want to do. The more important trick is to seize those opportunities when they do present themselves and make the utmost of them. "Then," as Faust suggests, "to the Moment I'd dare say: 'Stay a while! You are so lovely!' "

Live.

Don't worry about getting older. Worrying about missed opportunities is a waste of energy that ought to be reserved for the young. By now, you know better. All that you learn up to about age twenty, anyone can learn at any time. The stuff of the next few decades often cannot be taught but must be lived. Have a little reverence for things you can't see or understand, and then plunge ahead. Live.

Life is an SNL skit.

One of my favorite *Saturday Night Live* bits was when a character named Stuart Smalley, a mock self-help guru played by the one and only Senator Al Franken, would repeat the mantra "I'm good enough, I'm smart enough, and doggone it, people like me." What was funny to me about it was that, although he was supposed to be the counselor helping others, it usually ended being he who had to repeat the phrase to bolster his own insecurities and frail self-image.

There is some truth to the value of such a practice. One observation is that most of us could stand to lighten up a bit when confronting our own ghosts, skeletons, and artistic roadblocks. Laugh at yourself a bit more. Don't beat yourself up. "People like you." Doggone it.

Positive thinking.

I positively believe that positive thinking works. Perhaps a better mantra than "I'm good enough, I'm smart enough, and doggone it, people like me" would be: "Though I make mistakes I am worthy. Worthy of second chances, new opportunities, respect, and most of all, love."

You will have many second chances in your life. In fact, I would go so far as to say, you'll never run out of second chances while your heart is still beating and your lungs are still filling with air. Use one of them today. You are worthy of it. I'm positive.

Two D's for today.

Life is drama and dance. And that's okay.

Let yourself feel.

Shall we just decide here at the beginning of the month that none of us needs to be a martyr? You don't have to be. I don't have to be. Nobody expects it, asks for it, or wants it. If they do, they have issues, not you. Don't allow yourself to be the victim.

As you go about the process of releasing your artistic self, let yourself feel anger, frustration, fear, disappointment, but also happiness, joy, success, love. You don't have to run from any of it. In fact, all of those emotions are what you will use in your artistic efforts, just as you use them in the rest of your life.

You wouldn't expect any of your students to not feel a wide range of emotions, and although you want those emotions under some degree of control, you don't expect the students to have to simply buck up, suppress them, and ignore them. Neither should you.

⚊⚋⚊

Be not afraid of trying.

Many people block themselves from trying new things—from taking up a sport to taking music lessons or learning a new language—because they are afraid they will do it poorly. If it's good enough to do, it's good enough to do badly. You're right: You won't be good at everything. But your attempt will change you forever and for good.

Make goals. But live now.

Those five words probably don't need a lot of explanation. But here goes. I suspect that most of us have at one time or another been so focused on what's next that we forget to live in the here and now. It's a "check things off the list" mentality, and it happens most often when our lists seem overwhelming. "If I just get through this concert and the church service on Thursday night and the play this weekend, I'll have time for something I want to do." The problem is, those were all things you "wanted" to do, but you somehow forget. Consequently, none of the experiences are as rewarding as they could have been. They are just over.

This is one of those ideas that we must remind ourselves of once in a while, so that life doesn't get spent—it gets lived.

Unclutter.

Today is the day we begin to unclutter your life. Believe me, this is a struggle for me, too. I like to think my clutteriness is a by-product of growing up in a huge family in which frugality was essential. Things had to last. You didn't throw things away carelessly.

Now I'm an adult, and it is still difficult for me to get rid of things. However, I have witnessed the amazing amount of energy you and I waste searching for something in a heap of whatever. Or how many times have you found yourself trying five pens that don't work before you find one that does—and then not tossing those first five? Our time could be better spent if it wasn't so crowded and full of stuff.

Remember, our goal is to get ourselves into a position in which we can more effectively focus on the parts of life we have neglected. It's hard to focus with all this static, so today is a good day to start to clear the air.

Make a list.

At least once a month we should make a list of something. Some would suggest we do this every day, but let's get real. All we would be doing is making a list, and every list would start with "Make a list."

Nonetheless, we can handle once a month, so why not make a list of simple things you actually do. These can be very simple, but you still have to write them down. I can walk around the block. I can call a friend. I can make the bed. Success breeds success. The list of what you have done gets longer. Likewise, the list of what needs to be done gets shorter and less overwhelming.

The next list (and it need not be written today unless you're on a roll) will be at least three things you want to get control of in your life that will move you along on your artistic journey. I can free up Tuesday afternoon for a voice lesson for me. I can audition for the local community theater or chamber chorale. I can delegate the costuming of the holiday show to a parent.

At the top and the bottom of each list write "I can be a teacher and an artist in the same lifetime." Everything else on the list should help you achieve that goal.

Creative vs. artistic.

When you participate in an art-related activity outside of your own classroom, would you describe yourself as "an artist" or as "being creative"? Let me encourage you not to be afraid to use the term "artist" in describing yourself to others and especially to yourself. Being a "creative" person is fine but it seems ultimately more limited. There is a cachet that is associated with the word "artist" that you should embrace and perhaps even flaunt. If you are going to be in a position to advocate for the arts, promote the arts to others, involve more people in the arts, and teach the arts, then taking the time to develop your own artistic side is essential. If you see yourself as an artist, practicing your art and presenting yourself to others as an artist will raise your standing among your peers and your students.

You are an artist and you teach. It's a solid and valid combination.

—————

Make music.

You probably spend the majority of your out-of-classroom time on lesson planning, grading, fixing instruments, etc. But schedule some time to make music, too. You the artist/teacher will have a relationship with your students that is different from what you ever would have as exclusively a teacher or an artist.

I realize time is short, but when was the last time you gathered three or four other music teachers together and played brass quartets or sang some music you love? I had a group of college friends who continued to do this after we graduated and were out teaching. Most would try an instrument that they hadn't played much, in order to teach it better when they returned to school the next day. That was okay, but it is also important to play or sing what you do best in order to really feel as though you are making something with artistic merit, using all your previous training as well as learning something new. These can be incredibly rewarding experiences and, frankly, can make you a more effective artist and teacher.

What happened?

Someone nobody seems to know once said, "There are three kinds of people in this world: those who make things happen, those who watch things happen, and those who wonder what happened."

Most teachers I know are of the first ilk. They make things happen. But often they are so wrapped up in making things happen for others that they neglect their own needs and aspirations. Then they wind up in category two, where they watch others have all the fun—especially in regard to making art—or they are completely sidelined to the point of category three, where they look back at their lives and wonder, "What happened?"

I believe there may be times when it's preferable to have one foot in each of the camps (okay, two feet and one hand). There certainly is nothing wrong with being a watcher on occasion and even a wonderer once in a while. But if your goal is really to reignite the fire of the artist in you, you now need to take some of the time and energy you put into making things happen for your students and make them happen for you. Let everybody else watch and wonder at you for a while.

Teaching is art.

John Steinbeck—certainly one of the greatest American authors of all time—wrote in 1955:

> *"I have come to believe that a great teacher is a great artist and that there are as few as there are any other great artists. It [Teaching] might even be the greatest of the arts since the medium is the human mind and spirit."*

I include this here in the short, dark days of February to remind you that, although you may feel far from the core of your artistic self, at least one great mind believed that what you do every day is art.

Turn ordinary into extraordinary.

As a teacher and an artist, you have the opportunity to take what may seem like an ordinary life and live it in an extraordinary way. Most important, you are in a position to help others do so as well. The most extraordinary lesson you can teach—and it is taught best through your everyday example—is to live a life filled to capacity with wonder and love.

Time for a checkup!

A prescription for rediscovering and time-releasing your artistic self:

1. Give yourself a checkup.
2. Do you have a plan?
3. Are you acting on it?
4. Are you doing it with an eye on quality?
5. Check the plan again.
6. Administer the first dose.

Invest in someone else's quest.

You can often tell when certain people have had a lot of psychotherapy. They use the same buzzwords regularly. They spend a lot of time talking about and worrying about themselves. They have learned to protect themselves from what's hurting them. This is not a judgment, simply an observation.

Today is a day to not think so much about your quest but to focus on someone else's. You know of someone who needs the encouragement, release, loving kick in the pants, and so on that you sometimes need. Look around. You are surrounded by other wonderers who are on personal quests similar to yours. Today, look beyond your students to other adults. Today is the day for you to provide a gift to them. Invest in them. It's healthy. Someday they might return the favor.

Do the preparation for which your courage is worthy.

The entries for February 13th and 14th are related. So you can read them both today and take a day off, or read them both each day for review. It's your book and your quest, so do whatever you like!

Be daring. If you are going to make a change, you must have the courage to change your behavior. You can't expect to approach everything the same way and also expect something to change. You are brave, or you can practice being brave until it becomes a more natural part of you. Reward your courage with a plan of action.

Do the sharing that is worthy of your caring.

Be caring of yourself and others. It is essential that you take care of your physical, mental, and spiritual health in order to bring your best creative self to the canvas or the stage.

Then, give of yourself by caring for others. Share, through your example at least, the courage you have discovered in yourself to take care of yourself. Encourage those around you to do so, too. It's a higher calling. Make certain your art reflects that caring.

Bigger than yourself.

As a teacher, you have a community that is interdependent. It ought to also be a fraternity of encouragement and support. Look for that encouragement and support right where you are. Let yourself feed off your and your colleagues' common sense of purpose and higher calling, thereby allowing yourself to move forward as an individual and then beyond yourself as a part of this larger community. What role can you play in this community to help all of its residents benefit from that encouragement and support?

Fire away. Every day.

Somebody once said to me, "My, you write so much. You must do it all the time."

No, I don't. But I do write something almost every day. It's amazing how much accumulates. Not all of it is very good. In fact, most of it is not. But once in a while you hit on something. The thing I have learned, however, is that you never hit anything if you don't fire away. So, I encourage you to fire away every day in your art. Do a little or do a lot. It won't all be good and sometimes it will be way more or less rewarding than at other times. But fire away, and sometimes you'll hit a bull's-eye. (You might be the only one who thinks so. Art's funny that way.)

Surround yourself with attitudes of possibility.

There are plenty of naysayers in the world. You can't avoid them completely, but you don't have to give yourself over to them either. Through no scientific proof whatsoever, I will boldly assert that I think there are just as many people in the world who possess attitudes of hope and possibility as there are Eeyores. Perhaps because I spend my life around teachers and children, I know far more people of hope and possibility than Eeyores.

These purveyors of the possible are the ones who are going to solve the issues of our time, big or small. They are the ones who see light at the end of the tunnels and, if you let them into your life, will help you see yours, too.

We constantly exhort children to choose their friends carefully. We need to do so, too. Surrounding yourself with people who embrace and share attitudes of possibility might be the most effective move you can make in the pursuit of your artistic potential. They are not hard to find. They are the ones who are getting things done and seem excited by the world as opposed to worn down by it. Chase 'em down or let them catch you.

The value of mistakes.

Jazz artist Miles Davis is widely quoted as saying, "Do not fear mistakes…
there are none." The value comes in what you learned and what you
will do next.

Successful or significant?

Here's a good question to ask yourself: "Are your ambitions to be successful or significant?"

Most teachers I know, most artists I know, and most artist/teachers I know have no problem answering this question. They are interested in being significant. I suppose you could turn it around and say that if you achieve significance, then you are successful. Yes! Let's go with that. Set your heart on continuing to live a life and to pursue a career of significance, confident that if you are significant you will impact and improve life far beyond today. Teaching and illuminating the human condition through artistic endeavors will make you eminently significant, and I'll suggest successful, too.

Agents of change.

No artistic endeavor is inconsequential.

Changing attitudes, relationships, situations, or lives is a big job.

Teachers do it most of the time.

Artists do it most of the time.

Teacher/artists do it all the time.

Take time, my friend.

Taking time to pursue your art is not a waste of time, no matter the finished product. Focus on it. Plan for it. Live it. It is the process of art that illustrates the dynamic nature of what it is to be human.

The good news is that, unlike so much of the rest of your life, in many of our artistic pursuits there doesn't have to be a deadline. Make it last. This can be the part of your life that you stretch or confine to your timeline. Think more of the process of art as opposed to the product, and I think you will have a far more satisfying experience in the arts.

No standing still.

Use your artistic efforts to stretch and learn and grow. You're either growing or declining. Art and humans are dynamic. There is no standing still.

From paper to reality.

Forget about everything for a moment except what you would like to do if you had no responsibilities.

What prospect excites you more than anything else?

What do you do the best?

What do you enjoy the most?

What are you most confident about?

These are not necessarily easy questions and you may actually feel embarrassed about some of them. But it's okay. If you want to be an astronaut or a cowboy, it's fine. I've been there. Really. It's fine.

The much more difficult question is, "Now how should we get there?"

If you've written down the answers to these questions, the next logical thing to do is to write next to your answers one thing you could do to move in the direction of making your answers realities. One thing. It's a start. Like planting a tree. Twenty years ago or today.

To the moon and beyond.

If not today, sometime soon go someplace you have never been. It doesn't have to be far away. It might be a synagogue if you are not Jewish, a church if you are; a school locker room or laboratory you have never set foot in; under your desk; anyplace where you will experience something new. Keep your eyes and ears open.

It's so easy to walk the same path to work every day, or drive the same highway, have coffee with the same co-workers in the same place, go about the routines of the day after day after day. This is not totally bad. There is undeniable comfort and joy in having some things you can count on.

But growth and change must at times be forced or, at the very least, nudged. Try a new restaurant. Shop at a new store. Read a new author, listen to music you thought you never would give an ear to. But most important, go someplace new. See how somebody else lives, and open yourself up to being moved and changed by the unfamiliar.

Me? Them? Us?

Dreamers build the world; schemers erode it.

Have you ever met someone who always seems to have a new idea of how to move himself or herself up in the world through some trick heard about on late-night television or from a twisted podium or pulpit? People like this intend to get rich quick or achieve a premature promotion through something other than hard work and experience. These people do not use their gifts to make the world better. Instead, they wear away at the fabric of honor and respect that ought to bind us all together and make us better by one another.

As you dream about your reawakening artistic efforts, ask yourself this: "Who will benefit from my artistic endeavor? Me? Them? Or us?"

I have a strong sense that the work you put into efforts that benefit all of us will sustain you the longest and help you realize the significance of the life you have chosen.

How did they do it?

Read a book and try to figure out the author's artistic technique and process. Do the same when watching a movie, listening to music, looking at a painting. Then give yourself time to reflect upon it.

In other words, do what you did too much of in college. Analyze a work of art, trying to avoid for the moment getting wrapped up in how it does or does not move or enlighten you. Just study the mechanics of the thing. What were the actual steps that the artist took to make this "thing" happen?

A painter acquires the canvas and stretches it over the frame, then mixes the paints, selects the brushes, perhaps sketches the painting in pencil, and on and on.

Now, what are the mechanics of what you would like to accomplish in your field of art? Make another list of the real steps it's going to take, leaving out inspiration, motivation, emotion, and all of that. Just name the concrete "to do's." Now, let's figure out how to attack number one on that list and get started.

Make choices.

Make choices—then another choice, then another.

People say that for a writer the blank page can be very intimidating. On the contrary, to me it has always been pretty exciting—so full of possibility. The blank page is not so frightening if you just start making choices one at a time to fill it up.

When you are putting together a concert, you choose a concept, perhaps a theme. Then you choose a venue, then music, a cast, costumes, lighting, program, and on and on. The entire project is a series of choices that you make that eventually get you to the end product.

So, start making choices about how you might more effectively rediscover the artist inside of you. What's your medium? Music? What kind of music? Will you play or sing it? Compose it? Produce it? Record it?

Just start making choices and see what unfolds—knowing that things will change along the way, but that you're moving. No more paralysis. You're making art by making choices.

The beauty of a plan.

What is it you want to share?

Perhaps that should be the initial spark to your creative process in the same way it was a spark for your teaching process. You want your students to know what you know and to understand what you understand about your chosen field, so that they can appreciate what you certainly appreciate, maybe not in the same way you do, but with the eagerness that you do.

Now think about your art. What do you want to say? What do you want to create? What do you want to share? Answer those questions and you'll be a step closer to doing it. Just as in good teaching, you have to start with a plan, knowing you will veer from it on occasion, abandon it frequently, and rely on it every once in a while. The good news is that with your artistic plan you don't need the principal to approve it. It's just for you.

Leap year!
Huh. What's that all about?

Does February 29th really deserve a page? I suppose if you were born on it you would think so. Okay, here's a bumper sticker I saw and loved.

Out of my mind.
Back in five minutes.

See you in March.

Time for some steps.

March can seem like a long, dark tunnel. But the days are getting longer and the sun is shining more, so it's a good time to think about taking concrete steps to release your creative/artistic self.

The first thing might be to plan some professional or artistic development. Make a commitment today that this month you will:

- Go to at least one seminar related to your artistic quest.
- Take (not teach) a workshop or a class that will address your artistic endeavors.
- Travel to one inspiring place.
- Listen to one book or CD or podcast by someone who is on artistic journey similar to yours.

This may seem like a lot of commitment for one month. But it's a long month and an exciting opportunity to reinvigorate your artistic quest.

Be honest.

Be brutally, blissfully honest to your peers, your students, your family and, most important, yourself. It's okay. You can handle it.

It doesn't help to kid yourself about the predicament of your life. Many people say they want things to change but take no action or any real steps to make that change happen. When nothing new happens and they find themselves in the same confining situation a year later, they start looking for someone to blame instead of looking in the mirror and saying: "I'm in charge. If I really want things to change, it's going to be up to me."

Or maybe you don't really want things to change.

Just be honest. Then, don't beat yourself up about it either way. Live with your honesty, knowing that you can re-evaluate the situation as often as you like, change your mind, change your direction—or not. It's up to you. Honestly.

Sweat the small things.

In March I like to wallow in the madness of the NCAA basketball tournament. I spend a good chunk of my time in a little place called Los Angeles, and if you live in LA and you like basketball, you pretty much idolize a man by the name of John Wooden. Coach Wooden was the basketball coach for the UCLA Bruins when they dominated ten out of twelve seasons of March madness to win the NCAA tournament in the 1960s and '70s. This has never been done before and most likely will never be done again. Even if you're from North Carolina you've got to admit that ten championships in twelve years is pretty astonishing. In his career at UCLA, Wooden coached his teams to 620 wins in twenty-seven seasons and was named the NCAA's basketball coach of the year seven times. Quite simply he was the greatest coach ever.

Coach Wooden was full of wise sayings. One of my favorites is, "Do not let what you cannot do interfere with what you can do." So many great John Wooden stories have become a part of the lore of the basketball world, like how he would spend most of the first practice each year teaching his players how to put on their socks and tie their shoes to avoid getting blisters. He believed that attention to this sort of detail would make the difference between a good team and a great team. He sweated the small stuff and he made certain his players did too. It obviously worked. Can it work for you?

"Make every day a masterpiece."

John Wooden two days in a row. It must be that the madness of March has taken hold.

"Make every day a masterpiece." What an inspiring piece of advice for any of us who are on a journey to re-energize our artistic selves.

The average human being lives about 25,000 days. That may sound like a lot but, if you're anywhere near my age, you are already approaching 20,000. Suddenly 25,000 doesn't look like very many.

So there really is no time to waste. Today is the day to start. How can you make this day and every day after this a masterpiece? There ought to be a degree of urgency to your quest. Not a panic, but certainly a zest for going after "it." What's the worst that could happen? You fall short on some days. So what? Once in a while you might live a masterpiece.

—— 3/3/3 ——

Angle of repose.

One of my favorite books is Wallace Stegner's *Angle of Repose*. If you haven't read it, try to find the time to do so. It's stunningly beautiful.

What does this mean, "angle of repose"? Consider a rock tumbling off a mountain. Where it naturally lands and the angle it sits at rest is its angle of repose.

What is your angle of repose? For most of us, there comes a time in our lives when we realize that this existence we're leading was assumed as we fell off the cliff of life. All the bumps and tumbles along the way caused us to land in a music classroom or a studio, with or without a spouse and children, in a certain location in the world, and so on.

Unlike the rock that fell off the mountain, however, we have some control over our angle of repose. We can adjust it if we like or accept it as it is. Most of us don't really need to jump off another cliff and make ultradramatic changes to the life we find ourselves living. Most of us on occasion might need a nudge here or an adjustment there to make us more comfortable or at least happily accepting of our angle of repose. For instance, the little nudges that we take to help us rediscover our artist selves do not mean we should abandon all that we love about our life; instead, we should use them to get a different viewpoint or to relieve a weight-bearing point in our angle of repose that's feeling a bit too much stress. We are not taking a flying leap; we are simply but purposefully adjusting our lives the way we shift in a chair or roll over in bed.

A lesson from my mother.

March 6th is my mother's birthday so I dedicate this page to her.

Mom taught me many great lessons. One that I think is among the most important is the idea that we each have a responsibility to look after one another. You see, my mother was an only child who went on to have ten children of her own…in ten years! I was right in the middle.

Imagine when we kids were all six to sixteen years old. There were very few times when we were all home for dinner at the same time. Consequently, we had an unwritten rule in our house that at dinnertime we would all sit in our assigned places. After "We fold our hands and bow our heads…" and before the eating frenzy began, we would look around the table to see who wasn't here. Someone was always off to football practice, church choir rehearsal, or some other activity. At this point my mother would make up plates of food for whoever wasn't there and set the food aside so there would be something for the absent ones to eat when they got home. What we learned was that as humans it is our duty to look around and make certain everyone else is taken care of, perhaps even before ourselves.

Often it is good to think of others before yourself and see what that does to free you from the burdens of your own angle of repose.

Teaching is good for you.

Possibly one of the healthiest things about being a teacher—although in a sad way—is that you are often surrounded by children with issues that make your own issues seem insignificant. Teachers may suffer less personal angst because they see and share in the angst of so many other people.

While I don't intend to trivialize the travails of your own life, I believe that in a world of Twitter, tweets, and "all-about-me" mantras, teachers set the finest example of each human's responsibility to look after those with whom they share the planet. Furthermore, teachers who reflect this care and concern in their own artistic efforts significantly amplify that fine example.

Be calm.

In a debate, calmness is a sign that you are confident of what you are talking about. In debate, even if you aren't feeling it, be calm.

In your artistic journey, calmness will help you remain focused on your ultimate goals as you remember that you are doing this for yourself, not anybody else. If there is stress, you are causing it. So stop it.

Making changes in your life is nothing to panic about. There really are no deadlines in your process of getting back in touch with your artistic self. Having no deadlines should help to reduce stress that gets in the way of the process. You set your own time frame.

You have enough stress in other parts of your life. Working on your artist self is the fun part. Be calm.

Be good-humored.

A good-natured sense of humor shows you are comfortable with yourself. In a debate, a sense of humor is a sign that you are confident of what you are talking about. In debate, even if you aren't feeling it, be good-humored.

In your artistic journey, a sense of humor will help you remain focused on your ultimate goals, as you remember that you are doing this for yourself, not anybody else. If there is stress, you are causing it. So stop it. Keep smiling.

Making changes in your life is nothing to be grumpy about. There really are no right or wrong answers in your process of getting back in touch with your artistic self. That there are no wrong answers should help to reduce the stress that gets in the way of the process.

Working on your artist self is the fun part. Be good-humored.

Be good.

Sometimes I think we educators get bogged down in the daunting higher mission of the whole profession. My opinion is that our profession is so full of absolutely amazing and dedicated professionals, who are so well trained and passionate for what they do, that it can be a little intimidating. Let me suggest that we don't let that get us down but rather let it pick us up. You are part of this remarkable group that helps shape and save the world one student at a time. You don't have to be remarkable. Just do good: good work born out of genuine goodwill.

Now, can you transfer that as well to your artistic enterprises? You don't have to be remarkable and neither does your art. You don't necessarily have to *be* good. Just *do* good.

No pain, no gain. Ha!

I think the adage "No pain, no gain" is rather bogus. So there.

As teachers, our attention to the process is often more important than the end result. The process need not be full of pain. It may be challenging at times, but not painful. Perhaps it's just the way you look at it.

I often tell young performer wannabes: "If you don't like rehearsal, get out of show biz, because you are going to spend a whole lot more time in rehearsal than you are in performance. If you don't genuinely love the process of getting there, you sure are wasting a good chunk of your life doing something 'painful' just for a few minutes of bliss."

Personally, I'm a rehearsal guy. In most cases, I get a bigger kick out of rehearsal than the actual performance. I like to do it over and over and feel it get better and better, or at least more comfortable and rewarding.

So focus on the process of your art more than the end result. If it's that painful, change the process. There's "gain" in knowing when to change courses.

Have a good time.

In the Talmud, it is written,

> "Man will be called to account for having deprived himself of the good things which the world offered."

Teacher. Artist. Rabbi. Don't beat yourself up. The world is a beautiful and bountiful place with much to be relished.

Travel lighter.

I'm a rabid traveler. No, I don't have rabies from traveling. I have a passion for traveling. If there is one lesson that I have learned in all the many trips all over the world, it is the value of those two words, "Travel lighter."

Let me suggest that most of us would do well to travel lighter even if we never left home. Rid yourself of the baggage of life; the stuff that makes it more difficult to move through the world with fluidity and ease.

Getting rid of "things" will be easy. You can wear only one pair of pants at a time, so how many pairs do you really need? Okay, I guess you could wear more than one pair, but on most occasions there really is no need. Lighten the physical load.

But it is even more important to lighten your emotional load.

Nobody expects you to take on the weight of the world. You can't and shouldn't. Examine the responsibilities you assume and ask yourself which really are your responsibilities and which are imagined. To feel the freedom to be artistic might astonish you, once you realize that everything isn't your fault.

Be hopeful.

(Perhaps my favorite poem.)

Hope is the thing with feathers

That perches in the soul

And sings the tune without the words

And never stops at all.

Thank you, Emily Dickinson.

Hope. It's the most important thing you have to offer your students, your peers, your colleagues, your family, and your world.

What's missing?

We are halfway through a very long month. It's time for some tough questions. We're friends. You can handle it. I challenge you to write a short answer to these five questions.

Ask yourself:

What is missing in my life?

What have I put on hold?

What am I waiting for?

What would fill my heart and make me happy?

What would I regret if I died tomorrow?

Look at your answers. Now, let's tackle one of those today. It might be simple. It doesn't have to be earth-shattering. You might have many answers to some of these questions. Pick an easy one or pick a hard one, and get started.

—3/3/3—

A belief is just a belief.

A belief is a belief is a belief. And sometimes beliefs need to be re-examined. You are free enough and strong enough to question everything you have ever believed. You are free to acquire new perspectives. You won't die from it. Or even go to hell.

Many times the things that hold us back artistically are things that we have been told and that we never had the courage to question. So, we feel guilty because we want to dance. Question your most core beliefs. Are they propelling you forward to a more fulfilled life here on earth or boxing you into such a narrow path that your need for artistic expression is being squashed? Have the courage to question, doubt, and even challenge. If you are just going to regurgitate what you have always been told, then what do you really have to say as an artist?

An artist must at the very least have the courage to question what he or she believes. Even if you come back to the same conclusions and embrace the same beliefs, you will not be the same, and neither will your art.

"It's sad not to know. It's tragic not to want to know."

Have you ever used that saying, or something akin to it, on your students? It's not the most upbeat and affirming statement in the world, but it's a good challenge to those who say they don't care about learning something new.

Of course you know what's coming. I have to ask, "What about you?" Are you avoiding going to workshops, taking a class, sending your work for publication, or pursuing a new interest because it seems like a lot of work or you are nervous about the outcome? As teachers, we often talk about the goal we have of making our students lifelong learners. Yet, are we setting a good example for them if we do not demonstrate our own curiosity and lifelong pursuit of knowledge?

None of us is too old to learn something new. "You can't teach old dogs new tricks" is untrue. I know an impressive number of grandmothers who are on Facebook. Today, explore some area of your art that you know little about and see what doors might crack open. You want to know.

The value of "no."

I'm a strong believer in the value of the word "no." I believe it's a word that may not be used enough at home or at school. Mostly, I believe in the value of "no" when it comes to parenting and training students. If you don't set the boundaries, you can't expect a student to stay within them. Every time I hear of a teacher getting an award for outstanding work, the students interviewed always say, "We love him/her." The next thing they say is, "Oh yes, he/she is very strict." Students appreciate rules and guidelines. You don't have to say "yes" to everything to be a positive teacher.

Now, how about the "no" word in regard to your own life? Have you have become bogged down with an ever-growing list of responsibilities, all of which you have said "yes" to even if you never uttered the word aloud? You need to start using "no" to give yourself room to breathe and grow. It's true! There may not be as many lights on the classroom Christmas tree this year. There may be a shorter program with the youth choir this month. You may not be able to provide music for the ladies luncheon every third Tuesday and you sure won't bring them homemade cookies. But, by saying "no" once in a while, you may have time to work on your own personal development as an artist. That growth will make you a better teacher and a more effective participant when you do say "yes."

It's a journey.

Finding fulfillment is a journey, not a happening. The process that you are undertaking by making lists, trying new things, meeting new people, traveling outside your comfort zone, and so on are all a part of this joyful and continuing experience of artistic fulfillment. It is good to remind yourself that the journey will never end. Unlike putting on a show or painting a picture, there is no final end product after which you begin the next project. It's just you. Beautiful you on a journey toward joy and fulfillment—yes, in the arts, but also in life.

Junk in! Junk out!

There is a lot of junk in the world. The people who say "God didn't make any junk" do not get cable television. Be aware of what you eat, read, listen to, or watch. The negativity and fear that is spewed on us from all angles is a poison that can skew our hearts and minds and steer us away from the joyful pursuit of artistic expression or even a joy-filled life. Be skeptical of the reasons that people say or write what they do. You are smart enough and brave enough to discern for yourself right from wrong, honest criticism from baseless blather, helpful dialog from venom.

If all you read, watch, or listen to day in and day out are twisted tales of doom, gloom, and judgment, how in the world are you ever going to express yourself from a "junk"-free frame of mind?

Turn it off. Then go listen to Vaughan Williams' "Fantasia on a Theme by Thomas Tallis" and remember how beautiful the world really is.

Go ahead. Wear the cheesehead!

Don't wait until you're old to wear a purple hat. I do get a kick out of those groups of women I see once in a while at a luncheon or on a bus heading out for a naughty day in their purple hats. When I say "naughty," I mean they all have these beautiful smirks on their faces that say to everyone, "I read that book where that lady said 'when I'm old I'll wear a purple hat' and now I'm doing it and everybody can talk about me all they want 'cause I'm old, I'm brave, I'm eccentric, and thank God there are a bunch of other ladies here with me so I don't feel completely foolish because I am, after all, a lady." They make me smile.

But perhaps we shouldn't wait until we're old to be a little naughty like that. Put on your purple hat today, or your cheesehead or your Afro wig or your feathered boa, and let yourself be talked about. It'll set you free.

Happy birthday, Stephen!

March 22nd is Stephen Sondheim's birthday. I'm sure you are aware of that and wore an appropriate costume to school today. Perhaps the Demon Barber of Fleet Street or John Wilkes Booth suited you well.

As far as I'm concerned, it should be a national holiday in his honor. In fact, let's just declare it. Oh, nobody listens to us anyway, do they?

Well, he is my favorite so I salute him today and include in this book an appropriate line for all teacher/artists who may fear the blank canvas ahead or the shadows on the path of uncertainty. As Stephen would say through the mouth of Dot, one of his best characters in *Sunday in the Park with George*:

> "Move on. Stop worrying where you're going, move on.
>
> If you can know where you're going, you've gone.
>
> Just keep moving on."

Ah! Thank you, Mr. Sondheim, and happy birthday.

FEE.

I often talk to young performers and tell them that there is a F-E-E that accompanies the privilege of having an audience and that without attention to these three facets of their art, they may be giving their adoring public less than they deserve.

F is for FOCUS. For singers this means not only the placement of the voice but also visual focus. Where is their attention? Can they use their own attention to focus to help the audience focus?

E is for ENERGY. There is a gap between the audience and the performer. Physical, yes. There it is, in the form of an orchestra pit or a stage's apron. There is also an emotional gap, best closed by the practiced energy that a performer exudes. It's your job to bridge that gap, not the audience's job to come to you.

E is for EMOTION. Perhaps this is the most important element of all. For what is art if not for the emotional response it induces? Agree or not, it's worth considering.

So now, what parts of this FEE can you use to jump-start your artistic self? Certainly FOCUS. Identify the steps toward your goal and take the first one. ENERGY: It takes a concerted effort to take that first step. EMOTION? It's okay to be angry, giddy, gloomy, determined, and so on. It's not okay to be neutral. Pay the FEE.

No shortcuts.

Here is another obvious admonition I offer up to young artists on their own artistic journeys: "There are no shortcuts to success. It just takes good, not hard, work."

It's true, it seems, that for some people art comes easy. They may be blessed with a natural gift that seems to ooze from them with little effort at all. But even they are not reaching their full potential if they are not doing regular, good work toward bettering their craft, honing their skills.

For most of us, the work of making art ought to be an ongoing, disciplined venture with methods even to our madness and regular attention to the skills that enable us to make a contribution.

Get a life!

I have just been visiting an overseas private school full of dedicated teachers, terrific and hardworking students, and sincere parents, more than a few of whom are obsessed with the success of their particular child. These parents spend their every waking day and night working, campaigning, cajoling, and politicking to make certain that the dreams they have for their children are realized. (Notice I did not say "the dreams of their children are realized." These are not always one and the same.)

To these sincere but somewhat misguided parents, I want say, "Get a life—your own life." The best way to instill in your sons and daughters a passion for learning, and to encourage them to have the courage to pursue their dreams, is for you to model what it is like to live a life of passion for learning as you pursue your own life goals.

As artist/teachers, we need to get a life as well: our own life that embraces our role as teachers facilitating our student's quests to fulfill their dreams, and as artists who demonstrate regularly what it means to live the full life of the artist within us.

—————

You are the hero.

I think it's interesting that in our society we look regularly for heroes to come along and rescue us from ourselves and what we perceive as our unfulfilled lives. It might be a new president, a charismatic religious leader, a wise guru, a teen idol.

Let me boldly suggest instead that, in the end, you are the hero you've been waiting for. This is not to say that you should abandon your relationship with a Higher Being. But within that relationship you should look to yourself to make the changes that you want in your life, not to the latest fad on television or the latest political pundit or even a thumping voice on the radio.

Your relationship with a Higher Being may help you. I believe it can. With that help, you can take the practical day-to-day steps that can rescue you from your artistic stalemate. You're the hero who can move yourself step by step in the direction you want to go.

What's so great about career anyway?

Esa-Pekka Salonen, the former director of the Los Angeles Philharmonic Orchestra, quoted Pierre Boulez in an interview published in the *Los Angeles Times*, and now I quote them both:

"Pierre Boulez used to say about career, 'I don't know what it is. You can't eat it; you can't do anything with it. Career is useless. Music matters, and career is a by-product of music making.'"

"Yeah, but you gotta eat." (This is me editorializing.)

Salonen then added: "But of course the best thing about so-called career is freedom. I don't have to do anything that I don't find artistically interesting. And so having got to this point in my life I also know what I enjoy and I know what I will not enjoy.

"These," Salonen said, "are the only two good things about getting older."

Well, I think there may be a few more good things about getting older, but I think his point should be well taken.

Is your "career" helping you do the things you want to do artistically or is your career a hindrance? The goal is to use one to help the other. If one side or the other has completely taken over, maybe a balance of vocation and avocation is what we really are striving for here. One can help the other if they are given equal time and energy. How is your balance? What can you do to equalize it?

Be confident that you're making a difference.

According to those wise figures in our March 27th entry, career is important for the opportunities it affords you to pursue whatever else interests you most.

But thinking about career, it may be a good time to stop asking "How high will I rise?" or "How far will I get?" and start asking "What difference will I have made?"

Embrace the enormity of the challenge it is to be a teacher and the huge burden of responsibility that is inherent in the task. You know you are making a difference. That may be as far as you need to get regarding career. The world has been changed because of you and your commitment to your students.

THAT is a reality a teacher can count on. That's your capital to spend. Will the value of your artistic endeavors do as much? Perhaps yes. Perhaps they may do even more. And perhaps not. But you can pursue them with the confidence that your influence is guaranteed as a teacher. You've earned the opportunity to play risks in your artistic life that you may not want to do in your role as educator. How fortunate to be able to take an artistic risk, not knowing how it will impact anyone or anything, but confident that, the next morning, you'll be back making a difference in the most noble career on the planet.

Put yourself in your dog's "shoes."

Try to imagine the good feeling it must be to be petted and scratched by one who loves you. Enjoy the moment and the ability to get out of the confines of your own soul and to experience the soul of another. Even if it's your dog's. Perhaps especially if it's your dog's!

It can be very satisfying and empowering.

Be comfortable.

At times it can be tempting to look at your colleagues, family, or friends and think that maybe you should be more ambitious, not settle for the routine of your life, do more and do different.

There may be times when you should. But try not to punish yourself for being comfortable where you are. You have chosen a noble profession and you do it very well. If you enjoy it and are fulfilled by it, relish your career comfort as opposed to fighting it.

Still, almost everybody's life could use a little tweak here and there, which is why the self-check you are doing by reading these daily missives might trigger those nuanced changes that you sense you need. This should be the fun part. You are not in a position of having to throw the baby out with the bathwater even if all those around you feel the need to do so for themselves. Revel in the fact that you've made a meaningful career choice, are good at it, and are experienced enough in it that you can turn your attention to areas that you feel you've neglected—such as your art. What a strong position to be in!

—∼◊∼—

Hope springs eternal!

It's the last day of March. Somewhere it HAS to be spring! And with spring our thoughts turn to gardening. Well, at least mine do.

Here is a fact. Teachers, gardeners, and artists live long lives. I have no scientific evidence or studies to back this up; I just know it.

My friend Roger's mother, in the words of a widely quoted proverb, suggested that all you need in life are three things:

Something to do.

Something to love.

Something to hope for.

Gardeners, teachers, and artists have all of this.

To do: Come on, do I really have to make a list?

To love: Flowers, color, music, children…

To hope for: Fruits from their labors. Beautiful, dynamic, edible, forever, or ephemeral, this is the stuff for which we rise every morning.

Do all of this: Garden, teach, do your art. Live long and prosper. It's spring.

No fooling!

Don't wait for someone else's permission to believe in yourself.

I realize this sounds a bit like a Hallmark card. So be it. We all seek approval from our peers, our friends, colleagues, parents, even our own children. It's natural to do so. But a healthy dose of self-confidence is nothing of which to be ashamed and is essential to pursuing your artistic goals.

Obviously, at one point in your life you felt you had something to offer in the arts. That's why you studied your art and even chose a career in it. You rightly believed, "I have something to offer." You probably felt this even before you found you had that special gift that meant you could also teach. You took piano lessons, sang in a choir, studied some other instrument, tried your hand at painting, sculpture, acting, writing, something. Now, you have to remind yourself that you still have that gift. It never went away even if you might have strayed from it. So, think about what those early experiences were like. You didn't need someone else to tell you whether or not you were good at it or at least had something to offer. You knew. Their affirmation was a bonus.

So know again. Believe that that very young artist is still in there and has a right to come out. Then, let it happen.

⸺◈◈◈⸺

Show them courage.

We worry too much about whether we are going to be any good at "it." We were once. We believe we were once. What if we can't do it anymore?

Not only that, you have built a reputation on being the expert in this field over your years of successful teaching. What if you decide to get up in front of a crowd and sing a solo, for instance? What if you don't do everything that you're always trying to get your students to do: Sing with proper breath support, be on pitch, make it look easy, and so on?

We think, "Will I be making a fool of myself or, worse yet, show the world what a fraud I really am?"

Real and genuine fears; real and genuine nonsense.

By example, show them the courage it takes to stand up and try something that scares you. Show them the courage it takes to not be very good every time but to keep growing and learning and showing up. Keep working at it and, next time, be better. You know what it takes to get "there." It's not all raves and successes. It's step by step, and the best lesson you might teach them is that you just have to keep doing "it."

That was then, this is now.

I can do it differently.

Today is a brand-new day, and everything up to this point was just rehearsal for your next act. Open the curtain and let's get on with the show.

―〜〜―

Stop asking; start asking.

Stop asking:

"How high will I rise?"
"How far will I get?"

Start asking:

"What am I doing with my life?"
"What does life have in store for me?"
"What difference will I have made?"

Last day on earth.

If you feel as if this might be your last day on earth, well, it might be. Might as well do the dishes. You'll feel better and the kitchen will be cleaner.

Someday it *will* indeed be your last day on earth. This is nothing to be afraid of. The realization of this fact may instead help you muster the courage to live every day as if it may be your last, giving your all as a teacher, an artist, and all that it is to be uniquely...you.

Exercise.

Some people love it. Really! They do! They are so lucky. Some people hate it. You might be one of them. Do it anyway. Nothing will do more to release your demons, your creative blocks, and your artistic spirit than vigorous, regular exercise.

I have heard that you are supposed to get your heart rate up for 150 minutes a week. That's a lot. I hope you do it, because I think it is good for everybody's physical well-being. But I almost hope more that you do it for your emotional and psychological well-being. I believe so strongly in the power of physical activity to cure or soothe our emotional pains and fire our creative juices. When I get grumpy, I go running or I dance. It helps so much. When I need inspiration for a song, I go running or I dance. It's amazing to me how the rhythms, melodies, and even lyrics flow when my body starts to go. See, there's a rhyme right there!

Love it or hate it. Just do it.

Write it down.

When you wake up in the middle of the night or in those fuzzy hours just before dawn when you are not quite with the actual world, what do you consider?

I sleep with a pencil and pad on the bed stand. Nowadays, I sometimes use my PDA like a Dictaphone, but usually in the quiet of the morning even my own voice singing into my iPhone can ruin a lovely moment.

So I keep the pen and pad handy and sometimes I write down some idea that pops into my head just as I'm waking up. If I don't, the idea often flits away and I can't even remember the subject matter once I've brushed my teeth. Sometimes, later I'll look at whatever the idea was— a lyric, a thought for an article, plot for a play—and I'll realize it was the dumbest idea I ever had, and I've had some dumb ones. (Did I tell you I once ran for Congress?)

Often those early-morning ideas do seem reasonable at the time and are goofy a little later on. But, once in a while, you hit on one that's actually worth remembering. I'm always thankful when I've made the effort to get a reminder down to help me create at a later time. I highly recommend it.

~ 2/2/13 ~

Yes, you can!

You have choices. You do have choices. You know "I can't because…" is a copout. You know you can.

Make an exercise of writing down the reasons you feel your artistic life has stagnated. "I don't have enough time." "I might not be any good at it." "It will take away the time I need to devote to my regular job." "I'll be neglecting my family." "I can't afford it." Write down whatever you think is standing in the way of your "going for it."

Now, dispel those excuses with solutions. Write down next to each how you will handle it, knowing that where there's a will there's a way, and that you are about to make the way.

You will be better in all you do when you feel free to be completely who and what you are. Your friends, family, colleagues deserve a fulfilled you. So do you.

Embrace it.

Embrace the life that is handed to you and make something of it. Don't run away from it, apologize for it, or rue it. Live with it and rejoice in it. Remember that it's still developing.

You might wish you were 6 foot 8 and lived in Buckingham Palace. But you aren't and you don't.

Take of stock of all that you are and where you've landed. Now be honest about what things can be changed and what cannot. You can change your location. You can change your schedule. You can change your priorities. You can change your attitude.

You can't change your height or move in with the queen.

Embrace the beautiful life that is handed to you and make something of it.

If there is goodwill in your efforts, the efforts are good.

I believe that this is essentially true. Whatever the results of your efforts as a teacher or as an artist, if your motivation and energies are targeted to the betterment of human kind, it is an effort worth putting forth.

So, what is your motivation for teaching?

What is your motivation for pursuing your art?

The fact is, you have chosen two arenas, teaching and doing art, that have enormous potential to do good. You know that the arts can heal and nurture like nothing else. You know that the arts can illuminate the human condition like nothing else. You know that the arts can inspire us all to do better by one another and by ourselves.

The arts can also do a lot of harm. The same energy that can be used to lead people toward the light can be used to lead them to the dark recesses of the human spirit.

You made a good choice. You are a teacher and an artist. If there is goodwill in your efforts, then rest assured that your efforts will be worthy and good.

No box.

Try not to imagine that you are boxed into a corner. At least three of the walls of your world are open to you. The wall you lean upon is the life you have lived. It's solid and can't be changed. What happened yesterday or yesteryear is behind you. It has helped make you what you are today but it doesn't have to determine what you will be tomorrow or for the rest of your life.

Look forward to the open walls with paths that lead to a bright and exciting future. You can walk through any one of those walls and down new paths of possibilities knowing that a solid wall is behind you—not holding you back but pushing you ever forward.

Change it up.

If your artistic/creative well seems to have run dry, ask yourself, "What have I been filling it with?" Then start refilling it with new experiences: Read a different kind of book, go to a different kind of movie than you would normally choose. Visit a different art gallery. Eat in a unique restaurant. Research people who do something like what you want to do.

If you always read the same kinds of materials, eat at the same places, or walk or drive the same routes, how can you expect new revelations that you can use in your art? You will be a more effective teacher and artist if you change it up.

Embrace collaboration.

Surround yourself with creative people. I am one of the kings of collaboration. In fact, other than perhaps this book, almost all of my projects are collaborations of one kind or another. I write musicals in which I collaborate with other composers or arrangers. I stage productions where I collaborate with lighting designers, sound engineers, costumers, dancers, actors, singers, and so on. I love collaborations because everybody brings their gifts to the table and we all get to indulge and try to come up with something that we could not do as well by ourselves.

Look for someone with whom you can collaborate on an artistic project outside of your regular job. Maybe you want to write a song or a play. Perhaps you want to mount a recital or an art showing. Express to someone you respect your desire to try a new artistic endeavor. Set aside some time for a brainstorming session on what kind of project that might be. With that first collaborator, make a list of who else you might involve and what the ultimate goal is, aware that the goal might change dramatically as you continue to collaborate.

Artistic collaboration is not for everybody. There will be strong opinions, egos, compromise, and so on. So, be careful to choose collaborators whom you respect and who respect you. Keep an open mind as the collaboration develops, realizing that the end result may not be exactly what it would have been had you done the entire project yourself. That's what collaboration is all about and it can be incredibly rewarding.

No right. No wrong.

There is no right or wrong in the art you make. It is simply what you create. It's yours, right? It's your expression through the arts. Consequently, don't be afraid that the message of your art may not be everybody's cup of tea. You might not even like it in the end. But own it. Then try another one that may more accurately say what you were trying to say in your previous efforts.

The arts are such a wonderfully dynamic endeavor. As you produce art, you have the opportunity to make a statement in so many ways and about anything that you have an idea about. Don't worry that your next artistic statement might contradict what you have stated through a previous work. That's okay. You are dynamic, too, and ever-changing as an artist and a human. In fact, art changes people, both the artist and the consumer of the art. That's one of the big reasons to do it.

No right or wrong. It's yours.

Tax Day. I'm just sayin'...

It seems appropriate that on Tax Day I say a word about dollars or lack thereof. I firmly believe that most people think they need more money than they do. This feeling that they don't have enough makes them afraid of trying new things, especially things like the arts, an area in which very few of us will ever get rich.

Of course, I'm not talking about having enough money for the basic necessities of staying alive (food, clothes, shelter). But how much do you really need?

I'm always amazed at people, particularly students, who tell me how broke they are as they hang their heads down so that they can gaze at their $200 tennis shoes.

Now, don't get all huffy and say I'm out of touch. All I'm suggesting in this little missive is that if you are using your lack of financial security as an excuse to not pursue your artistic dreams, maybe you should re-examine how you are spending what money you do have. You have to choose your priorities. I just happen to think that $200 tennis shoes are a funny choice if it means you can't do art.

If none of this applies to you, skip this page. I'm just sayin'...

Plan what's next.

Oscar Wilde, truly one of the great wits of all time, wrote,

> *"In this world there are only two tragedies.*
> *One is not getting what one wants, and the other is getting it."*

I suppose he's warning us to "be careful what you wish for." But for the sake of this book, his admonition might be a wise reminder for several other thoughts to consider.

What if all you ever wished for happened when you were in your twenties? What are you going to do with the next many decades? I think that we all should have dreams and goals that fit in the inevitable passage of time. Our goals at nineteen ought to be different from what they are at thirty-nine or sixty-nine or ninety-nine. At each of these stages of life we should also be planning what is next when/if we reach this goal. As creative people, we should have something we've just finished, something we are in the thick of, and something that is germinating in our minds and hearts, ready to be the next thing we are "in the thick of."

Creative people never run out of dreams and ideas. But we do run out of time.

—⟨⟩/⟩/⟩⟨—

Choose kindness.

Whom do you admire more, clever people or kind people?

It's just a question. But it's one that is worth a ponder on a day in April. Someone did ask it of me once.

My suggestion that people could be both kind and clever received a smirk. But I believe it is possible.

In the end, being kind is more important than being clever. Few would deny this. But if you ever find yourself in a situation where you have to choose, I recommend kindness.

Even as you approach your art, the honesty that accompanies true kindness will give substance to your work and make it worthy of a life of its own.

Who's got your back?

Find people in your life who can help you make the most of your successes and your failures. Surround yourself with those who will push you toward excellence with honest opinions but always with your success and well-being as their fervent wishes for you.

Without being paranoid, examine the people around whom you are spending your life. If they are not helping you be the best that you can be, spend less time with them, or invest enough in that friendship to have the honest conversations about what you need and expect from a friend, colleague, or family member. Make certain that they have your success and happiness as a goal of theirs. Then, of course, make sure that you return the favor.

Press on!

"Nothing in the world can take the place of Persistence. Talent will not; nothing is more common than unsuccessful men with talent. Genius will not; unrewarded genius is almost a proverb. Education will not; the world is full of educated derelicts. Persistence and Determination alone are omnipotent. The slogan 'Press On' has solved and always will solve the problems of the human race."

—Calvin Coolidge, 1932

Think big.

Sometimes you have to take a big leap. You can't jump across a big ravine in a couple of small hops. Think about that for a minute and consider what big step you need to take to get your creative self up and running. Think big—outlandishly big. And prepare yourself to take that flying leap.

Adjust your dreams.

You have more than one idea in your head and more than one dream in your heart. Try not to be limited by too narrow a dream or too narrow a mind. You are capable of so much more. This goes for your art as well as your walk through life.

There will be artistic projects and ideas that you have not even thought of yet. Keep your heart and mind open to them; you never really know how they may morph. Also, one idea, although it may be your goal, will almost always lead to another dream or idea. Stay open to the dynamic nature of life and art. Be willing to adjust the best dream you ever had to one that is even better. Be ready for new discoveries as you reach and even surpass each goal.

Look up! Not down.

I sincerely hope that as a teacher you have encouraged your students to look up, not down, on one another, on strangers, on their world, toward their future. I hope that you do so, too.

As you dive into your newest artistic challenge as well as your everyday life, I hope you approach it with a loftiness of ideals and ideas that boost those who come in contact with your efforts. I hope your art is never used to tear the world down but to lift it up.

Art can set the tone for the kind of world we all want to live in. Art ought to be used to light us up.

What an exciting role to play!

Fore!

In the spring many folks get wrapped up in the excitement of the Masters Golf Tournament. I like golf. I'm terrible at it and it has ruined many a fine walk for me, but nonetheless it can be a nice way to spend a few hours out of doors.

My sister-in-law Mona Vold wrote a wonderful book called *Different Strokes* about the early days of women's professional golf and the lessons these amazing women taught through their example of smarts, dedication, and athleticism. Mona and I recently had a conversation in which we were trying to decide whether golf was actually a sport. It seems the young women on the golf team she coaches are often chided by participants in other sports as to the merit of a sport in which you don't time after time run head-on into your opponent causing each of you permanent brain injury.

After much back and forth we agreed that although golf is a sport it is also so much more. The mental and even mystical nature of golf in many ways allows it to rise above an ordinary game. In the study and play of golf, one is both an athlete and a prospective Zen master.

Similarly, you are a teacher, but you are so much more because you are an artist as well. You are an artist, and you are so much more because you are a teacher as well.

Practice.

In Mona Vold's book *Different Strokes*, about the early women involved in professional golf, she quotes the incomparable Arnold Palmer in his description of the Zen-like nature of golf:

> *"You hit the ball. You go find it. You hit the ball. You go find it. You hope you can sink a few putts."*

This is not unlike the work of a teacher/artist. You show up. You teach. You do art. You show up. You teach. You do art. You hope you enlighten some minds. You hope you make some art.

Here's another sagacious quip, attributed to many golfers over the years: "It's a funny thing; the more I practice the luckier I get."

Of course the golfers were talking about golf. For you the teacher/artist perhaps the thought should be, "The more I practice my art the more of an artist I become."

—⁓⁓⁓—

The pursuit of happiness.

We Americans are often obsessed with our God-given right to "the pursuit of happiness." Whatever that is! For some it is, of course, the pursuit of making money. For others, the pursuit is one of making a difference in other people's lives. There are as many definitions for the happiness we are all pursuing as there are citizens in this great country.

Let me make a suggestion. Perhaps if we were all not so busy "pursuing happiness" and slowed down, happiness might have a chance to catch up with us.

This is not to say you shouldn't look for new opportunities and challenges, and you definitely shouldn't just settle for the status quo if you are dissatisfied with any element of your life. But on occasion it might be helpful to look around, count your blessings, and realize that you really don't have it so bad. Maybe then your pursuit can be gentler on yourself and the people around you. Maybe then happiness will land on you as a butterfly lands on your shoulder.

Go be it.

It's hard to pursue a dream if you never had one in the first place.

Listening to the radio, I hear a folksy kind of song that goes something like, "Decide what you're gonna be and then go be it." Sounds like good parenting advice or something you might have emblazoned on a T-shirt, but to be frank, it's probably pretty sensible advice.

I'm not sure it is valuable to make your artistic goals and dreams so specific that there is no room for adjustment. Who knows what will happen along the way to change what you're going to "be"? But it helps to have an idea of what and where you would like to be at any stage along your way to "being."

That being said, some elements of your quest ought to be completely non-negotiable; honesty, courage, integrity, and passion come immediately to mind. I'm sure you have others you would add as you strive to "be what you're gonna be."

━━◁3/3/3▷━━

This is the fun stuff, right?

Keep your perspective.

You're making this journey because you feel it will help fulfill you as an artist and as a human being. But don't get overly dramatic about it. No one is going to flog you for how it turns out.

You want to reignite your artistic self.

You might be out to save the world. I hope you can. But let's start by making an artistic contribution right where you are today, with all the safety nets that surround you, including family, friends, colleagues, and even students who will protect you when you stumble. Later we can try the high-wire acts if you feel ready.

This is the fun stuff, right?

Get real.

Get real. This is the day of tough love. Actually, I don't like that phrase that much. Tough and love are two words that just don't seem as if they should be next to each other. What does it mean anyway? But, let's "get real" about your skills, and make the decision that you are going to keep improving those skills until the day you die. Learning and honing your teaching skills did not cease once you had done it once or twice— I hope. Instead, you are constantly working to learn new tricks of the trade, considering new discoveries made through others' research and how you might use them in your own teaching situations, and so on.

Likewise, when it comes to your artistic pursuits, it's time to "get real" about the time and effort it will take to pursue them at the level you find rewarding. You may have to give something else up. Are you willing to do that? You may have to sign up for a class, take a workshop, meet with a tutor, and rearrange your workspace—not to mention your schedule. If you're serious about making some changes, "get real" about what it's going to take to pursue your dreams. You can do it. You know you can do it. But will you?

If you get real about what's needed and still want to move ahead, I think you will take the steps to get the journey started.

———

Dance like...

I've never been crazy about that saying that frequently appears on candles: "Dance like nobody is watching." Really? Are you really more free and expressive when you are all alone? Are your greatest works of art a reality only in your private moments?

Come on. Many of us got into the arts partly because of our love of audience and the unique moments that happen when artist meets audience and vice versa. Do you have something to say in your art?

Then dance like everybody is watching and applauding.

Go see the world.

Get out an atlas or a globe. Spin it. Figuratively or actually, spin it. At the very least, imagine someplace you want to go on that globe. Now start to take the steps to go there.

I'm not sure I could think of a better way for you to awaken your artistic spirit than to travel someplace outside of your usual haunts. In fact, I'm obsessed with traveling. Here's why.

Every time I go on a trip, and I've gone on a lot of them, I come back a different person. Better? Worse? Who's to say? But, never the same.

Go see the world. Listen to its music. Taste its food. Marvel at its wonders. You'll be changed forever and for good.

Noah's Ark

If April showers bring May flowers, they also bring floods. Of course the greatest flood of all time was literally biblical in proportion. Don't build an ark just yet, but I dedicate the month of May to the greatest flood survivor ever, Noah. To begin, then, a song I wrote with my friend and collaborator Mac Huff, based on a child's simple prayer.

The Sea Is So Wide

Dear Lord, be good to me. Dear Lord, watch over me.
Dear Lord, hear my prayer.

The sea is so wide, my boat is so small.
Dear Lord, I stand amazed at the wonder of it all.
Adrift on a rolling sea with no guiding star in sight.
I feel so alone in the darkness of the night.

What I need is your hand. Will you walk by my side?
And see me as I am, my arms are open wide.
We can hope and we can dream for the dawning of a brighter day.
Dear Lord, be good to me and help me find my way, I pray.

Lost in the stars that glow thru' the blackness of night.
Each star is blessed with a wish of radiant light.
Like so many stars,
There are so many people whose dreams need a spark to shine.
If I stumble will someone hold on? Falling stars are forgotten by dawn.
Will someone hear my cry? Will someone ask the world "why?"
Will someone take the time to watch the sky?
Dear Lord! Dear Lord! The sea is so wide, my boat is so small.
Dear Lord, I stand amazed at the wonder of it all.
So shine your light throughout the world and bring me home to stay.
Dear Lord, be good to me, this is all I ask, and all I pray.
Dear Lord, be good to me.

Noah's Ark – Lesson 1: Don't miss the boat.

I recently came across an insightful view of lessons learned in a study of the story of Noah's ark. The original author of these simple but brilliant observations is unknown. I heard them in a speech by my treasured friend and role model Marian Wright Edelman. Now, with our own twist, let's examine Noah's lessons as they pertain to our quest for creative and artist invigoration.

Lesson 1: Don't miss the boat.

That's right. You can sit, stand, lie down, or stew about your dilemma, or you can do something about it. The water is rising. I suggest you start building.

———

Noah's Ark – Lesson 1: Don't miss the boat, Part B.

We are still on Lesson 1 in the month of Noah's ark. The crux of the lesson: You do not want to be left behind.

Everyone who did not get on the ark perished. I'm not suggesting that you are going to die if you don't pursue your passion for doing art with the same vigor as you approach your teaching. But you might drown in your own frustration and sense of pointlessness if you don't try your best to save yourself by getting on board.

But what is this ark you are supposed to board?

It's the ark that supports all your desires to participate in the arts. It's the ark you see boarded by others who are taking classes, attending seminars, and seeking counsel from colleagues and friends to help their aspirations as artists stay afloat. Don't watch others *carpe diem* and resent them. Get on the boat and set sail on your own wide-open sea.

Noah's Ark – Lesson 1: Don't miss the boat, Part C.

Life is short. Now that's a grand statement you didn't need me to tell you. Life accelerates—at least for most of us. You knew that, too.

You've got so many days and you want to make the most and the best of them. If you hesitate for any reason—fear, shyness, insecurity, exhaustion—the boat is not going to wait for you. It's leaving the dock (or the mountaintop) and you absolutely need to be on it.

You can talk to the captain later about switching courses. That's fair. But get on board, for you have everything to lose if you don't and everything to gain if you do.

Be brave. Noah was.

Noah's Ark – Lesson 1: Don't miss the boat, Part D.

If you are to thrive as an artist, I believe that you should recognize that something larger than just you is out there.

I believe that God believes in us.

I believe that God wants artists to succeed.

I believe that God wants artists to help awaken the rest of the world to the reality that they are a part of something bigger than themselves.

I believe that God wants you to not miss the boat.

Noah's Ark Lesson 1: Don't miss the boat.

Noah's Ark – Lesson 2: "We are all in the same boat."

Although you may think you are the only teacher/artist who has hit a brick wall or just felt bogged down in the day-to-day routine of his or her job, you are not. In fact, very few artist/teachers have not felt that way at one time or another.

Does that knowledge help you cope with the anxiety this feeling is causing you? It ought to. Because we are all in the same boat, we are also there for each other. Throw somebody a lifeline when you recognize his or her dilemma, and there most likely will be a lifeline for you when you most need it.

There is comfort in knowing that, although your life path is different from any that has ever been traveled by anyone, there is very little completely new under the sun. Read, watch, bear witness, and listen to the others in the boat with you. Be open to their experiences and advice. Then, sort it out to help you make the choices that are right for your journey.

Noah's Ark – Lesson 2: We are all in the same boat, Part B.

Since we are all in the same boat, help is all around you.

Sometimes you don't need very much, just someone to listen to the questions that are in your heart. Sometimes you need someone to set you straight, pat your back, buck you up, and be gentle with you.

Those people are here in the boat with you. They may be professional counselors, or they may be colleagues, family, or friends. Seek them out and value their help. Be grateful for their help.

Be honest with them about the journey you are on. They won't be able to figure it all out for you, but they might keep you afloat until the rain stops and the clouds clear.

Noah's Ark – Lesson 2: We are all in the same boat, Part C.

One of the challenges of all being in the boat together is that it might be easy to simply wait for some other passengers to give us the answers to our artistic dilemmas.

An artist cannot be passive. You have to go after it. Take charge. Be proactive instead of waiting to be instructed.

The other passengers in the ark have their own concerns. They'll listen. They'll advise. They can support, encourage, praise, and prod. But in the end, you have to trim the sails, rev the motor, or row.

Noah's Ark – Lesson 2: We are all in the same boat, Part II.

Like it or not, as an adult you realize that there are always going to be others in your boat. You don't live on this ark by yourself. The good news is that you don't have to live with the fear that some artists have: that for some reason you will eventually find yourself alone, abandoned by most, or burdened by others.

You have chosen a profession, teaching, that is all about relationships with others, both students and peers. Similarly, as artist you have chosen to participate in a community in which you need never feel abandoned. Artists are some of the greatest commiserators I know. We love to share ideas, fears, doubts, triumphs, and failures. Share your boat with other artists. Be there for them when they need you and they will most assuredly be there for you when you feel a leak in your vessel.

When I think about Noah's ark and the animals that teamed up to join him, I often consider my favorite African proverb: "If you want to go fast travel alone. If you want to go far travel together."

Noah's Ark – Lesson 3:
Plan ahead.

It wasn't raining when Noah built the ark!

Take the steps now to be ready to lay the groundwork for your next artistic project. It all gets back to preparation: strengthening skills and talents that you already have, and concentrating as well on areas in which you feel inadequate.

Complete these two sentences:

1. "The areas of my art that I feel the most adept at are....."
2. "The areas of my art that I feel least prepared for are....."

Now consider the practical steps that will make the answer to question number 2 shorter.

Noah's Ark – Lesson 3: Plan ahead, Part B.

Planning ahead also implies "Do it now!" True, it wasn't raining when Noah built his ark, but he knew what was coming and he knew he had to prepare for it right away in order to deal with it when the downpour came.

For you the teacher/artist, today is the day to start preparing for the artistic experiences you know lie ahead for you.

Okay, if your schedule this semester is so jam-packed that you can't possibly fit in time for your own art, don't beat yourself up over it. And for heaven's sakes, don't whine about it.

Instead, look forward to that bright light at the end of the tunnel and do what is necessary (change your schedule, drop something, alert people who need to know that you will be making some changes, etc.) so that when this semester is over you are prepared for your new angle of repose.

Noah's Ark – Lesson 3: Plan ahead, Part C.

Some might suggest that change is difficult. Noah suggests, and I agree, that not changing is more often a lot more painful than change. Resistance hurts.

As teachers/artists/human beings, we are dynamic or we're dead. Changing your life in small or big ways should not be frightening or painful. Resisting change might be.

Be human. Change it up. Prepare for the reality that your life as an artist will always be in flux, tacking to and fro like a boat, or an ark, on the open sea.

Get ready. Things are going to change. Thank goodness.

Noah's Ark – Lesson 3: Plan ahead, Part D.

You have one life, one opportunity to make it meaningful. Don't wait until the next go-round to do what you want to do. Do it now.

This doesn't mean abandon all and gallivant off to a cave in Delphi to ponder your navel. Or maybe for you it does!

What it means for most of us is to start today taking the steps necessary to live your artistic life to its fullest. I'm not suggesting you abandon your role as teacher. You can do both and you should. But, start immediately to create an atmosphere and practical scenario that will allow you to concentrate on that area you feel has been neglected, the area that is causing you anxiety.

Start today. Tomorrow is today and it's starting to sprinkle.

2/2/13

Noah's Ark – Lesson 4: "Don't listen to the critics and the naysayers."

If Noah had listened to all who told him he was crazy, he and his family would have drowned with all the others.

If you're so worried about what others might say or think, you will never do anything. Man up. Woman up. Artist up.

Do what you feel you need to do as an artist to fulfill your dreams, not someone else's.

Noah's Ark – Lesson 4: Don't listen to the critics and the naysayers, Part B.

Try not to be too easily bruised. Artists, as vulnerable as they often are, have to develop fairly thick skin when it comes to their critics, and there will always be critics.

If you haven't developed a pretty resilient coat of armor already as a teacher, you probably aren't teaching anymore. Just because someone doesn't like your artistic statement doesn't mean it isn't worthy. It's your statement, no one else's.

Every, and I mean every, great artist has had hits and misses. But that doesn't make the effort unworthy.

Personally, I can tell you this. Some of my own most self-fulfilling artistic adventures were not the ones most appreciated by those who came in contact with them. But for me as an artist, those adventures are still the ones that, as I consider them in hindsight, were the most rewarding to me.

Do your art to please and express yourself. Let the critics and the naysayers do what they do: Criticize and naysay. You move on to your next project.

Noah's Ark – Lesson 4: Don't listen to the critics and the naysayers, Part C.

It's pouring. Forty days, forty nights. Noah says, "Beware the wet blankets."

Have you ever found yourself so excited about a new artistic adventure, or any kind of adventure for that matter, only to have someone close to you squelch it with disparaging words or one roll of the eyes? I know that if you teach middle school you have!

During this "coming out" phase of your process, it may at times be wise to keep some of your dream and your plans for it to yourself or revealed to a very select few. There will be plenty of time later to share the result of your efforts, should you choose to, with everyone in your life and the world at large. Right now you don't need any wet blankets to put out your fire. Should they try, remember to keep it in perspective and recall Noah's Lesson 4, Part B: Don't be too easily bruised or dissuaded from your rightful pursuit of happiness.

⸺❀⸺

Noah's Ark – Lesson 4: Don't listen to the critics and the naysayers, Part D.

Sometimes you have to go through rough waters in order to reach a calm-enough sea that will allow you to sail on in tranquillity. Although it is Noah's example that suggests that we don't listen to critics and naysayers, there are people in this boat with you who might have good advice to help you find the smooth sailing. Be open to the good advice of friends and colleagues. You will know the difference between criticism that comes from someone who genuinely wishes for your happiness and success and criticism from someone who not-so-secretly relishes your demise. Be open to good people, and good ideas may often follow.

Noah's Ark – Lesson 5:
"For safety's sake, travel in pairs."

Although Noah's Lesson 5 may in some ways seem contradictory to Lesson 4, it is not. Lesson 4 warned us to ignore the critics and the nay-sayers. These people missed the boat, remember? Lesson 5 reminds us that partnering with others who have goals similar to ours, in this case artistic growth and survival, can be a wonderful tool to help the boat move forward.

Brainstorming with positive survivors can be so helpful and rewarding. Travel with fellow artists. Seek them out. We are different.

Noah's Ark – Lesson 5: Travel in pairs, Part B.

Since you are one half of the pair, be careful that you do not become the naysayer in this relationship. Your success or failure as an artist has nothing to do with the success or failure of your travel partner or partners.

I often say to young people, "It is easy to be a friend to someone whose life is falling apart. You can let him cry on your shoulder, bring her casseroles, be a hero and confidant. The more difficult challenge is to be a good friend when everything is going right in your friend's life and perhaps not in yours. When a friend's art comes easy. When he finds success. When she wins the lottery. What kind of friend are you? That is the real test."

As fellow artists we choose collaborators to help us celebrate the days when art flows easily and encourage one another when progress inevitably has its slow days. As often as you can, try to play the role of positive motivator to your partner artists just as you do in your role as teacher to your students.

<hr>

Noah's Ark – Lesson 5: Travel in pairs, Part C.

As you travel though life with all of the other pairs, it may at times seem crowded. There may not always seem to be room for you and your art.

There is *always* room for you and there is *always* room for art.

At times you may actually have to slow down to let it develop. Don't rush your art by setting deadlines and don't set yourself up for disappointment by setting your goals unrealistically high. This is not to shortchange yourself. This is to say, relax. Don't burn yourself out as an artist just as you do not want to burn yourself out as a teacher. Let the art gently flow. This is not something you have to conquer. This is something you have to love.

There will always be room for love.

Noah's Ark – Lesson 5: Travel in pairs, Part D.

As you search for just the right artistic partner with whom to board the ark of artistic survival, make certain to choose a companion with whom you feel safe.

Of course, not all artistic projects are collaborations. But many are. For me, some of the most rewarding have been.

It is crucial that your artistic partner and you share a mutual respect for each other as artists and as human beings. Be careful not to fall into the trap of looking for a partner simply to fill in the gaps you feel are missing in your own abilities or training. There may be some of that. But that kind of relationship can easily drift into the category of "using" one another as opposed to true collaboration.

The animals that boarded the ark were equal partners. If you choose to collaborate, look for a partner who can sometimes serve as editor, muse, realist, constructive critic, and so on. But most important, choose a partner who makes you feel safe in this daring adventure.

Noah's Ark – Lesson 6: "Remember: The ark was built by amateurs, the Titanic was built by professionals." (Feel your power.)

You may on occasion feel out of your league as a teacher and as an artist. It's true that there will always be someone with more training, perhaps even more obvious God-given gifts. So what?

One of the many wonderful things about being a teacher is that you are almost always working with amateurs. You are surrounded by people who are just now learning the skills and exploring the crafts that will be with them for their entire life. Most of them will continue as amateurs, but others will perhaps become proficient enough to make a career of something you introduced them to.

The art those students create as amateurs under your tutelage is as valid as anything created by the greatest professionals in the field. True, it may never make it past the refrigerator door or the No-Purpose Room stage, but art, amateur or pro, is a process, the process is legitimate, and the end result is neither right nor wrong—it's just the result.

Noah's Ark – Lesson 6: Feel your power, Part B.

Feel your own power. Don't wait for someone else to deliver it for you. Especially don't wait for the "experts" to tell you that your efforts are worthy, or not.

Sometimes I think we all believe that if we study long enough and hard enough, practicing art, that someday we will become artists.

If you are practicing art, you are an artist. You may get better at it. You may be more satisfied with the work once you have more experience. But, the act of doing art is what defines an artist. No apologies or explanations necessary. Just keep doing it, you artist, you.

Noah's Ark – Lesson 6: Feel your power, Part C.

Give yourself some credit. Very few people have trained for their professions as long as you have. Look around the table at your next faculty meeting. How many of your colleagues started training for their chosen fields when they were five or six years old, as you did? (Remember those piano lessons or ballet slippers?) You have been training for your teaching job and doing your art practically as long as you have been alive. You are an expert. Not to say there isn't more to do and learn, but you have a good head start and your ark is very much afloat.

Noah's Ark – Lesson 6: Feel your power, Part D.

Give yourself some responsibility. I hate to use the word "blame," but if I must….

If you are having an artistic block, realize that you are to blame. Nobody did it to you. Consequently, you have to be the one to remove that block you constructed.

But how?

By doing your art. Sit down and play or write. Pick up a brush, a pencil. Put on your dancing shoes and do art. Five minutes today is better than nothing. Use your own power to free yourself and get over the hurdles that haunt and taunt you. You are capable, immensely qualified, and ultimately in charge. That's got to feel good!

Noah's Ark – Lesson 7 (the final lesson): "Build your future on higher ground."

Art is powerful. There have been those throughout history who have tried to use that power to bring themselves up and the world down. This is not for you.

Teacher/artists recognize the good that involvement in the arts can do in the lives of students, the community, and themselves. Let goodness be your goal, and embrace the higher calling of a teacher and an artist to lift us all.

Use your art to work for a more peaceful and beautiful world. Use your art to create light, rather than darkness, unity rather than division, hope rather than despair.

―⸗⟨3/8/8⟩⸗―

Noah's Ark – Lesson 7: Build your future on higher ground, Part B.

Teach your students to look up, not down, and use your art to do the same. It is too easy to use the power of the arts and your role as a teacher to lead your minions astray.

I believe that those teacher/artists who embrace the higher nature of their calling will find they have fewer creative blocks and more energy to keep producing. We are on a mission: to teach and create, to entertain, enlighten, and elevate, yes, especially elevate.

With the power of the arts comes huge responsibility to make the world a better place. That does not mean that every song has to be "Zip-A-Dee-Doo-Dah" (although, man, I wish I had written that one!), or that every painting has to be rainbows and dancing fairies. Sometimes the darkest painting can reveal to us something about ourselves as humans that can help us move on in a more illumined state. Edvard Munch's masterpiece The Scream comes to mind.

The higher Truth that art can lead us to is its most valuable role. And that Truth is always up.

Noah's Ark – Lesson 7: Build your future on higher ground, Part C.

Be forgiving of yourself. There is no value in kicking yourself for what you perceive as wasted opportunities. Some might suggest here that plenty of others will kick you when you're down and that you don't need to do it yourself. I personally don't believe that.

Most people want others to be happy and fulfilled, just as they want to be. Most people live on high ground and we teacher/artists are welcome there.

Now is the time to set course on a new adventure. Today is the day to begin to build the ark that will carry you and your teaching, you and your art, you and your life forward. The ideas are buoyant when led by a moral compass that points to higher ground. Follow it.

Noah's Ark – Lesson 7: Build your future on higher ground, Part D.

There is no value in jealousy.

In the arts there is always room for everyone. There is unlimited room for another poet, composer, painter, writer, dancer, dreamer.

Art is not a contest. Your work need not be judged alongside the next artist and found worthy or not. It is all worthy. Work hard to rise above pettiness and gossip in life, in teaching, and in your art.

You might say, "But jealousy just happens. I can't help it." Actually, yes, you can. But, just like art itself, it takes practice and sincere effort.

Build your ark on higher ground. Make yourself worthy to be called an artist.

Landing Noah's Ark

The story of Noah and his ark is a transformational one. From the months or years of planning and choosing collaborators, to the effort it took to ignore the critics and the naysayers, to the realization that we are all in this boat together, and finally to the acceptance of the call to practice life on higher ground, Noah has lessons for all of us and, perhaps especially, for those of us who float around in the arts.

I strongly encourage you to consider again and again the lessons of Noah and how to apply them to your own life as a teacher and as an artist.

1. Don't miss the boat.
2. We are all in the same boat.
3. Plan ahead.
4. Don't listen to the critics and the naysayers.
5. Travel in pairs.
6. Feel your power. (The ark was built by amateurs, the Titanic by professionals.)
7. Build your future on higher ground.

Amen.

Come to shore.

I begin and end this lovely month of May with poetry. And since Noah has been our friend all month long, why not continue our sailing theme? Here are the lyrics to a song I wrote with my dear friend Audrey Snyder. It's a song about coming home.

If you have ever stood at the shore of the sea, you know it can produce feelings of awe and wonder, courage and nostalgia, joy and humility. If it causes you to think about that artist within you that seems to have gone out of your life for now, it may also produce intense feelings of longing—longing for that part of you to reappear. When it does, you will be there ready to nurture and celebrate, embrace and accept it, in the same way the father greeted the long-lost prodigal son with perhaps the greatest words ever spoken to a weary wanderer, "Welcome home."

Come to Shore

Come to shore. Come to shore.
You have drifted far too long.
Borne aloft in sun or gale, heed free of siren's call.
Come to shore. Come to shore.
Forswear your Field of Reeds.
Your Mama needs you now, your Papa needs you now,
Ah wanderer, I need you most of all.
Come to shore. Come to shore.
The dark sea shrugs its shoulder,
and its rush, like breath comes in,
and lifts you nearer to me.
Come to shore. Come to shore. Come home.

First: Be accountable to yourself.

When you're working with students, I expect that you regularly encourage them to be first and foremost accountable to themselves. Oftentimes we are our own best judge and, just as often, our own worst critic. In other words, we grade ourselves lower than our critics might.

The point is that student or teacher/artist, you shouldn't be pursuing your art for anyone but yourself. And, you should be the only one to judge your artistic efforts in the end. Like those students, you'll probably be more demanding on yourself than anyone else anyway, and the grade you give yourself is the only one that counts.

What grade do you give your art? Not very important.

What grade do you give your artistic effort? Crucial.

—— 2/3/89 ——

How are you growing today?

In order to live a life of art, you have to live an artful life. So, what are you doing today to help yourself live a life that is artful? Are you surrounding yourself with art and artistic people?

Look about and see the beauty of the world around you. Now, go out and see how that beauty is reflected by other artists at work around you. Then, go and try to reflect that beauty in the life you lead as a teacher and as an artist.

Bloom where you are planted.

Although I am a firm believer in the value of going off on adventures all over the place, especially outside one's usual comfort zone, I am also a believer in the "Bloom where you are planted" adage.

This is where you are. This is who you are. It's important to face that reality and live here in the moment in this very place. This certainly is not to suggest that the situation, as well as the locale, might not change. But you can explore your creative self and exert your artistic self, right where you are. You probably don't need to run from it. You probably do need to analyze it, see the beauty in it, and look for realistic opportunities right there, in the garden where you are.

A Buddha without a heart.

I once spent a year living and working in Japan. Take heed; I am one who doesn't take a year lightly. You only get so many. But my year in Japan was an enriching experience beyond measure that I wouldn't trade for anything in the world.

One lesson I learned there was the notion that anyone can build a statue of Buddha. Usually green in color, holding a scimitar, a club, and a shield, and riding on a carpet or an eagle pulled by lions, the statue can be made of jade or emerald, brass, or some other material. But until someone has given Buddha a heart, it is simply a statue and nothing more. It is the heart of Buddha that gives it meaning.

Now, I don't think it's a stretch to suggest that your art is similar. Whether it is a song you've written, a show you've produced, a painting, a poem, a dance, or a composition, until you have instilled in that work of art some genuine heart, it may be beautiful, but it is as impotent as a Buddha without a heart.

Questions and mysteries.

"Art is a lie that makes us realize truth."

—Pablo Picasso

"Ceci n'est pas une pipe."
("This is not a pipe.")

—René Magritte

"Look I made a hat, Where there never was a hat."
—Stephen Sondheim in his portrayal of Georges Seurat,
Sunday in the Park with George

"For what is art but for the Truth it sefls to reveal?"

—Johnny J.

Have you noticed I have so many questions and so few answers? I'm okay with that. Maybe you can be too.

Picasso and truth.

Let's consider Picasso a bit further.

"Art is a lie that makes us realize truth."

In 1923, after Picasso made this statement, he went on to explain:

"We all know that Art is not truth. Art is a lie that makes us realize truth, at least the truth that is given us to understand. The artist must know the manner whereby to convince others of the truthfulness of his lies."

As you consider your art, how will it reveal the truth? To you? To others?

When I was young I struggled with Picasso. I thought my mother would throw things like that out if I brought them home from second grade. Now I have come to realize that it is the anguish in those grotesque figures, or the beauty; it is the jubilation in the bright colors or the despair; it is the passion or reverence or, or, or…that is revealed and illuminates something to the viewer and makes it art. It helps us understand, at least "the truth that is given to us to understand."

Magritte and truth.

Let's consider Magritte a bit further.

> *"Ceci n'est pas une pipe."*
> *"This is not a pipe."*

Like Pablo, René goes further to explain his painting of a pipe with the above slogan beneath it.

"How people reproached me for it! And yet, could you stuff my pipe? No, it's just a representation, is it not? So if I had written on my picture 'This is a pipe,' I'd have been lying!"

Ya gotta love these guys! They are using their art to try to reveal the truth, as it is available to understand. You can paint a picture of a barn, or a tree, or a cow, but in truth you cannot say, "This is a barn, a tree, a cow." That would be a lie. Yet, the painting might reveal to someone what a barn, a tree, or a cow looks like for real.

Look for the ways your art can help reveal the truth, even though you know it's a big old lie.

Sondheim and truth.

Let's consider Sondheim a bit further.

"Look I made a hat, Where there never was a hat."
—Stephen Sondheim in his portrayal of Georges Seurat,
Sunday in the Park with George

This is the miracle of what you are embracing when you live the life of an artist. You can make something exist where there was nothing. A song, a dance, a painting of a hat. You are the creator revealing to the world what the Creator has revealed to you.

Is it a miracle? I don't know. I told you I have more questions than answers. Is it miraculous? If it isn't, it's darn close. Look! A hat where there never was a hat!

If that doesn't make you excited about a life in the arts, close this book and try something else. We have important lies to tell and countless hats to make.

—✦✦✦—

Johnny J. and truth.

Let's consider Johnny J. a bit further.

"For what is art but for the truth it sefls to reveal?"

Johnny J. was a nickname I acquired in college simply because my best friend was Johnny Scott and people needed a way to differentiate us. It stuck for many years. I included my own take on what Pablo P., René M., and Stephen S. were trying to say. It's fun to input your name in the mix. I once did a music workshop in which I followed Fred Bock and Moses Hogan. Try following Bach and Moses if you ever want a humility check!

What Johnny J. is trying to say is that Pablo, René, and Stephen were right. Art is about the search for truth. As an artist you have a dual role in the hunt. You search for truth for yourself as you practice your art and you help others in their own searches as they experience the results of your artistic efforts. This is an awesome opportunity. Don't put it off for another day. We need artists like you to help lead us all to truth and perhaps even to Truth.

What it is...is.

Live in truth. It's just a dent, a late flight, a disagreeable situation. But that's ALL it is. Just a little drama. You can handle it and get back to your real life...full of joy and hope and art.

Let me make a liar out of you.

Most of you who are reading this are probably music teachers, or you once were. So you know the power of music. As you stretch your artistic wings or vocal cords, use music to help you laugh, cry, feel inspired, comfort, relax, create, move on.

People use music to work out at the gym, help tolerate the pain at a dental office, soothe their grief, celebrate their victories. You, better than most, know that you can look into and listen to the music more deeply to actually help you clear your mind and focus your thinking. Really! Just as Picasso and Magritte talked about the lie of art as painters, we musicians are liars, too! Yay! And just as their lies help reveal to us the truth, so can the art of music, creating it, re-creating it, and consuming it.

It's the kids, stupid!

I'm sure you recall a certain presidential campaign that used the mantra "It's the economy, stupid!" to keep all eyes on the prize. I voted for that candidate, but the slogan bugged me.

For citizens and especially artists, I would change that quip around in a heartbeat from "It's the economy, stupid!" to "It's the kids, stupid!" Or, if you find using the word for a little goat to describe your tots offensive, you could chant "It's the children, stupid!" and it would suffice more politely. We'd solve a lot of problems in our world if we as adults stayed focused on what is best for our children more than what is best for us old folks. We've had our chance; let them have a go at it.

Focus on the children in your life. They can inspire and drag you along even when you think you can't move. Focus on their hope, idealism, vulnerability and, sometimes, brutal honesty. You think you can't keep going or try something new? Think about the children in your life, and get up and follow them.

Listen to your heart.

There is a rhythm in you. It beats in your heart. And I'm not talking figuratively. I'm talking about your pulse. I'm talking about your heart-beat, human!

I can't tell you how many times, when I have been searching for an idea for a song, that I literally listen to the beat of my own heart. As I get older, I'm just glad it's still beating at all!

What's surprising is that it changes. It isn't always a disco beat or a samba groove. But it makes music.

I'm not making this up. I write a lot of songs every year. Usually I have an assignment that will give me a starting-off point, a title, a subject matter, a style. If I need a fast-paced rock-and-roll song, I go for a run and listen to the rhythm of my feet and my heart. If I need a ballad, I go for a stroll and again I listen to my heart. Try it. And don't be afraid to skip, or pretend to skate, gallop like a pony, or leap like a gazelle. Others who may catch you doing so only wish they could.

Listen, I live on a ranch. I chop wood. I drive a tractor and a bulldozer. I shovel horse manure with a relish and, by God, I skip!

Listen to your heart.

Don't forget to breathe.

Tune into the rhythm of your breath and your heart rate. As we discussed yesterday, there's a music there to help you move on.

Often, when I teach a dance class, I have to remind my students to breathe. They get so excited, or they concentrate so hard on the task at hand, that they literally forget to breathe. This is not a good approach to life. It shortens it rapidly.

Take deep, slow breaths and consider the challenges ahead. You have the strength, and the oxygen, to deal with it. Panic won't help; breathing will.

———

Don't worry about who gets credit.

Often we are stifled by the honest feelings that all of our hard work as a teacher or as an artist is unrecognized. Goodness knows that a teacher's salary hardly makes up for the fact that we are ignored.

However, if you allow yourself to get bogged down in these feelings of lost respect or feelings of being unappreciated, your artist self is going to have a very difficult time feeling free enough to produce.

Of course, we all need positive reinforcement once in a while, and it is no fun to work hard and have your efforts taken for granted, ignored, or even—in some cases—resented. But if you allow yourself to be dragged down by this, the "it's not fair" abyss may just swallow you up. Instead, be your own best fan. You're an adult now. You know when you have done something of real value. You know when you deserve credit. Look in the mirror, be proud and, once again, move on.

Return the favor.

Since you have probably felt at some time or another in your life and career that you have been ignored or not properly credited with your good work, remember to not make the same mistake in reverse. Instead, look for opportunities and individuals that deserve your recognition and praise.

The wonderful feeling of giving praise and showing gratitude is a win-win situation. You help another feel the value of his or her work and you take your mind off any slight that may have happened to you, inadvertently or not.

Harboring feelings of having been slighted does no good for anyone, especially you, a grown-up artist.

Be a giver of praise. It will come back to you in spades.

Listen to Winston.

A way-too-often-quoted charge by Winston Churchill is the simple "Never give up. Never, never give up."

I say "too often quoted" only because good old Winston had so many clever and quotable words come out of his mouth, that to too often use this one seems a bit of a shame. Still, it's a jolly good message.

As a teacher I hope you never give up. "Never, never give up" on any student. Some will tempt you. But don't do it. Keep on keeping on. You just never know when the lightbulb might go on. You may never know about it, but you will know in your heart that you did all that you could do. Conversely, it will haunt you if you do give up on a student even if you never know what happens once he or she is out of your hair.

Likewise, as an artist, "Never give up. Never, never give up." Art is a process. Sometimes that process will seem easier than others. Sometimes you will feel success and other times utter failure. But keep on keeping on. It'll happen if you just listen to Winston.

Listen to Dorothy!

Okay, another quote to steer your course. I love this one by the late, great Judy Garland:

> "Be a first-rate version of yourself, not a second-rate version of someone else."

We all have mentors and idols we attempt to model ourselves after. Role models are valuable for people of all ages. Choose them carefully.

But in the end, you can't be anybody but who you are. Take all that came before you and all that are in front of you now. Put them in your heart and soul and be the best you you can possibly be. Teach that valuable lesson to your students and, as you start to re-emerge as the artist you are, confidently re-emerge as the most authentic version of you you can possibly be.

Get some "sassitude."

When I turned forty years old I got noticeably sassier. Well, at least in my mind I did. When you are young, oftentimes you are so worried that anything you say or do is going to follow you around for the rest of your life, haunting you, embarrassing you and your family, showing your obvious flaws forever to the world.

When you get a little older, you figure: "Hey, how much time have I got left? Might as well do what I want to do and say what I want to say!"

Whether you're twelve or a hundred and twelve, I hope you find the courage to be sassy (give it another word like "honest" or "forthright" if that suits you). It doesn't mean that you are going to quit being sensitive to the people with whom you share this planet and just say or do whatever you want. That would come under the category of selfish, and hopefully you left that back in seventh grade.

But, take this year to examine your true light. Don't worry what others think they know of you or what you may have convinced yourself of in the years up to now.

You are an artist. Show your true colors starting today.

—❦—

What are you sharing?

What you are sharing, not what you are getting, is most likely what you appreciate. We teach because we have a human need to share.

You started off as an artist, or an artist in training. But you found as you grew as an artist that you had an intense desire to share your love of that art with others. To do this, you became a teacher. This does not diminish your love for the art or your identity as an artist. You are a teacher AND an artist. Perhaps now you are simply at a stage in your life and career where you want to put more emphasis back on you, the artist. You want to get back to your first love, your art. But you still want to share it, precisely because you love it. So, you do both.

Two true loves. How lucky can you get?

You are more than...

Human beings are complicated creatures.

You are more than one thing. You are artist, teacher, sibling, parent, spouse, friend, fan, and on and on. If you can teach and have the opportunity to do so, you should embrace that as part of who you are. Likewise, as an artist (one who does art), you can work to dwell and identify in another sphere as well. These are not qualitative choices. Both teaching and being an artist are worthy passions that make up part of your whole identity. You can do it all without disparaging one over the other, or feeling that time spent on one area of your life is necessarily more worthwhile than time spent on the other.

Artist, teacher, and all those other elements that are you are mostly equal with one another if you choose to make them so. You can be a parent who also is a professional, a spouse who is also a sibling, a child who is also a parent, a teacher who is also an artist.

The mystery of talent.

Talent is God-given. Or, if you are uncomfortable with that statement, you might feel better with the idea that nobody really knows where talent comes from.

Success, on the other hand, is much less a mystery. It comes from drive and a desire to perform beyond the ordinary.

You have the talent. You have demonstrated that with the successes you have enjoyed in your life so far. You probably recognize that the most rewarding achievements have also been the ones where you worked the hardest, strove the most, tested your talents, and achieved something extraordinary. It wasn't easy. But it was worth the effort and was worthy of your talents.

Your God-given, mysterious talents deserve the effort it takes to do the exceptional.

Right, wrong...close.

As an artist and as a teacher, you have to be willing to think, question, and maybe even adjust your long-held beliefs and programming. This doesn't mean you won't come back to the same conclusions once you do, but you won't be the same because you had the fortitude to ask "Why?", "Really?", and "Am I sure?"

I might even be so bold as to say everybody should do that on occasion, but today I'm talking to artists and I think it is especially true for you.

As an artist you need to have the chutzpah to at least consider that the sky might not be blue, that people you idolize may have flaws, that Truth and truths are yet to be discovered. If you haven't the courage to do that, you will find yourself re-creating all that has already been imagined by those who went before you. You will not be making "new" but regurgitating someone else's vision instead of your own. Artists take a leap every time they approach their art, their environment, their life. It's about self-discovery, lest you find yourself less an artist than a copyist.

And that is my June 23rd lecture.

———

Right, wrong...close again.

I think this subject deserves another day of contemplation and exercise.

Can anyone ever be totally, 100 percent right? As an artist who seeks to reveal the truth through your work, how will you ever know if the "lies" you speak ever approach truth as opposed to drivel?

Here's the reality. Your statements of truth, as you interpret them, are just yours. No more. No less. The artist in the next room might have a different idea of what truth is and a different approach as to how to reveal it to the world. This ought not be frightening. This ought to be thrilling.

There is no shame as an artist in constantly re-examining what you perceive as right and what you consider Truth. As human beings, there is no shame in being a questioner. As teachers of the arts there may be no greater lesson you pass on to your students than your example of courage that says, "Keep searching for the big answers. Let art help you in your path to discovery."

The mirror to your soul.

George Bernard Shaw wrote:

"You use a glass mirror to see your face; you use works of art to see your soul."

Thanks a lot, George. I feel so much better.

Shaw did win the Nobel Prize for Literature in 1925 so perhaps he does deserve our consideration.

Have you considered lately how you want to use your art? As consumers of art we can look at other people's contributions to help us understand our souls and perhaps the souls of our species. But how will you use your art to help others see their own soul?

I have at least one simple suggestion. Each time you choose a piece of music to spend time on with your band or choir, each time you spend time with students analyzing a poem or a lyric, a painting, a dance, a symphony, consider whether it has an element that will help them see their souls. As you create or "do" art yourself, resist the tendency to do trendy, comfortable "classroom candy" and create something that reflects, like Shaw's mirror, what it is to be human.

What do you pray about?

What do you have? What do you think about? What do you pray about?

I have a bold assertion. In the end it isn't what you have but what you pray about that is really important. Okay, if prayer is not your thing, it's what you think about that's really important. Not what you wear, drive, eat, drink…but what you think and pray about that is everything to you.

Consider where your thoughts and prayers are and spend more time in your day-to-day life on those areas that are obviously important to you. It might help put everything else in its proper perspective.

Don't do it alone.

The very thing that makes us human is our interaction with other humans. Seek out human beings who have similar needs (that would be all of them) and desires (that would be other artists, at least) and make them partners in your quest to rediscover your artistic self.

I guarantee that you are not alone. In the end, yes, your art is personal and unique. But the journey has been made before, all the way until the very end. That's why we study the masters. Follow in the footsteps of those artists who have gone before you, who do almost what you'd like to do. Walk arm in arm with others in your generation who are on their own journey. At some point, and you will know, you will sense the time for you to forge your own path and be the unique artist you are. If life is 500 miles, the first 499 are laid out for you. That's when we learn. That's when we have fellow travelers. It's what you do with that last mile that will distinguish you. But you don't have to rush to the finish.

Your fear is talking to you.

"You'll make a fool of yourself." "You'll hurt someone." "People won't like me."

You're assuming these things. But are they based in fact or on your own assumptions? Perhaps once you recognize them as your fears you can rethink and free yourself from your own misconceptions.

"You'll make a fool of yourself." Yes, on occasion you will. Do not let that stop you. Live up to it by taking chances. Fools often are the best vehicles to lead us to the Truth.

"You'll hurt someone." Who? Your family? Your friends? You might. But people are more resilient than you think. Just don't leave them out of the loop as you go after your artistic dreams. They don't deserve your every waking minute and ounce of energy. They do deserve your sharing of the energy of this new venture. And they'll have your back when you need it.

"People won't like me." Some will think you've gone off the deep end. But the people who are really important will want what is best for you and not for an instant think of how it reflects on them.

<hr>

"I am going to do this!"

Yes, indeed, I think you are. We are getting close to the end of June. Soon little boys and girls will be standing on the end of diving boards with their friends looking up at them. Their little knees will be shaking. Their hearts will be pounding. They would give anything to not have taken that dare and climbed that ladder.

But, like you, they did. Now, here they stand, on the precipice of a new experience, a new day. As they approached the ladder they thought, "I am going to do this." Now they (you) are not so sure.

Do it. Jump. Pursue the art you want to pursue. Get wet. It might sting a little, but imagine the thrill when you come up for air!

Set your artistic GPS.

Do you have a name for that woman who talks to you in your car after you set your GPS? I call mine "Darlin'." Don't ask me why.

Now is the time to get a wee bit practical.

What do you want to accomplish or even pursue in this next artistic chapter of your life? If you could do anything, make anything, go anywhere, write, draw, dance, play, or sing anything, what would it be? Set some goals today. Otherwise how will you know which direction to head? Write them down. You can always change them.

Make some of them outrageous and some of them practical, or at least what seems practical to you. In fact, alternately make one goal simple and attainable next to one you consider far-fetched. Really far-fetched. This is just for you, and we are now beyond self-consciousness.

Punch in the GPS coordinates on the next chapter of your artistic journey and let the Darlin' voice, the one that is programmed inside of you, speak and lead you through the next phase of self-discovery.

It's not what you know.
It's what you don't know.

Don't expect to create your art by using only what you know. Pursue what you don't know—that's where art will come from. As an experienced teacher you learned that it was okay to not know everything. When a student asks you a question and you don't know the answer, you are confident enough to say, "I don't know. Together, let's find out."

Is it any different as you approach your art? Is it really art if you are just repeating what you or someone else has already done?

You will, of course, use your experience in your pursuit. But art will really flourish when what you create comes from an attitude of "I don't know what is going to happen or be created here, but let's find out!"

Who knows?

Do not be afraid of uncertainty. If you are, and always fall back on what you know and what you are comfortable with, you will never stretch any boundaries, never do anything new or unique, never go beyond the comfort of the familiar, and never be one who soared.

You have it in you. You've proved that time and again in the classroom. Now, demonstrate that willingness to fly out of the nest in your artistic life as well.

Perseverance.

If you're going to do this, you're going to have to be tenacious and mentally tough. Bring your determination to persevere to the worktable every single day. There will be days when ideas will come easy and you'll think, "This is a breeze!" And you'll ask yourself, "What was I afraid of?" There will be other days when you'll think, "I don't have an idea in my simple little head!" And you'll ask yourself: "What was I thinking? Who do I think I am?"

Persevere. Be willing to hang in there and stick to it when the going gets tough. The most successful people in the arts are not always the most talented, but the ones who keep showing up and keep at it. Keep at it. Tomorrow or the next day or the next, the breeze of inspiration will blow again.

——

Recess!

It's the Fourth of July and you might think, "Let's take a recess."

Go ahead. Play can be healthy and extremely liberating. Go watch a parade if you and your band are not already in it. Go to a park with family or friends. Have a picnic, play ball, take a boat ride, or swim in a lake. Play. It's good for you.

But as you have probably already noticed, just as being a teacher seems to never allow for a day off, neither does being an artist. For an artist, there's no shutoff valve. Your artistic sense just keeps being stimulated. I hope you're thinking, "Thank goodness."

Here's more good news. Those hours of play can be so stimulating that you may come back with a heart full of ideas of how to next be creative. The water in the pond, the float in the parade, the tuna in the casserole, the fireworks in the sky are all feeding you, the artist. Take a recess. You will never be the same.

Attention to detail.

It is the attention to detail that often makes the difference between good and great.

I frequently suggest to students that the difference between Disney World and all the other theme parks in the world is the attention to detail. When you visit the Haunted Mansion and stand in line, you are hemmed in by stanchions and chains as in any other park. But at Disney World the stanchions are topped with intricately cast gargoyles that give children and adults something to admire and rub their sticky hands on as they wait for hours in line. In Frontierland, the garbage cans are shaped like logs, and in the Main Street Cafeteria, when you get a butter patty on your six-dollar bun, it has Mickey Mouse ears embossed on it. Consequently, when people go home from Disney World, yes, they remember the thrill of Space Mountain, but there are other roller coasters. They remember the cuteness of Pooh, the smell of the popcorn, or the corny jokes on the Jungle Cruise. But what really impresses them is that someone took the time to put Mickey Mouse ears in their butter!

Pay attention to detail. There's a reason hundreds of thousands of people borrow against their life savings year after year to sweat it out at Disney World.

Aim to grow.

When you practice your art, be it playing an instrument, singing, dancing, acting, painting, or anything else, you do so not with the hope that you will simply maintain the level of prowess that you have already achieved. You practice to grow.

As you practice your art, consider before each repetition which part of it you are going to improve upon this time. Can you make the tone richer, the leg straighter, the line more expressive?

With each step you take on your artistic journey, aim to improve, not just maintain. Every repetition is an opportunity to do your art better and make the experience ultimately more rewarding.

Does reality get in the way of your dream?

Why is it that you lie in a hammock on a sunny July afternoon and dream of great things, and then wake up only to have reality destroy those wonderful dreams?

Perhaps we do it to ourselves.

Perhaps if we genuinely embrace our dreams—get out of the hammock and really pursue them—then our dreams can disturb reality and, because of our concerted efforts, actually come true.

Gratitude.

Express your gratitude. The summer months are an excellent time for teachers to do many of the things they simply do not have time or energy for during the school year.

Expressing your gratitude to those around you who support your dreams and your reality is a remarkably refreshing thing to do for them and for you as well. This is not taking attention away from your quest, but it is acknowledging that you are not on that quest alone. You have help all around you. Be thankful for it and express that thanks today.

Wake up!

Another thought about dreams. In order to make them come true there comes a day when you have to actually wake up and get at it.

What are the practical steps that you need to take to begin making your latest dream come true? (I say "latest" because artists will always have new dreams.)

Before you worry about Dream 2.0, identify Dream Number 1 and make a list of the steps you need to take to "get 'er done."

I will…

- Get up 10 minutes earlier.
- Get my supplies in order so that I can do the work of my dreams.
- Organize my space so that I feel in charge.
- Pursue a coach to help me get back into training.
- Sign up for a class or lesson that will help me get back on track artistically.
- Do my art every day for at least twenty minutes.
- Set up an area in my home in which I exclusively pursue my art.
- And so on.

Listen to Milton.

John Milton wrote,

> *"The mind is its own place, and in itself can make a Heaven of Hell, a Hell of Heaven."*

Who is paralyzing you from doing what you want to do? If it is happening, it is ultimately you. Okay…it's your mind. Recognizing that can be a wonderfully liberating revelation. Look to yourself to change your hell to heaven. Others will help you, but you and your mind are in charge.

"The trick to not being crazy is to not do crazy things." Milton did not say this. I did. If your life feels like hell and you are not able to spend the time doing and being the creative, artistic person you want to be, cut the crazy parts. Make a list of the things in your life that just seem crazy.

Do the things you have to do and the things you love. Let your mind, your heart, and your art change this hell into heaven.

Finding joy.

It is essential to try to find joy in the day-to-day. It is your right to do so.

This is a good time to try to analyze the little parts of life that you either take for granted or allow to irk you.

You are allowed to find joy in your first cup of coffee, your comfortable shoes, your morning walks. Save the drama for your art. Everything doesn't have to be over the top. Enjoy the little incidents and observations along the way and try not to let "big" decisions smother the simple joy that you—we all—deserve.

Creative thinking.

In the free world we claim to live in, we like to think that we encourage creative thinking. That is because we believe it is the creative mind that will find solutions to the great challenges of our world.

By teaching music or some other art form, you are helping the great problem solvers of the future discover their creative selves AND you are using your creativity to be a solution maker, too.

The world needs you to continue to do both: art and teaching.

———

Clear the clutter.

Earlier we talked about getting the clutter out of your life. We've all got too much stuff. Lighten your material load.

Now, let's talk about getting the clutter out of your brain and soul. Only when you have freed it from self-deception, delusion, and rationalization can you really be open to your creative self.

Be honest, most especially with yourself. What emotional and psychological roadblocks are in the way of your creativity? Who put them there? Remember, you are an adult and an accomplished professional. You put the clutter there and you can remove it. Lighten your emotional load.

Jumping hurdles.

What are the obstacles to your creativity?

Fear of criticism? Nobody likes to be criticized. But if that fear is stifling you to the point of not allowing yourself to move forward, you are letting those critics run your life for you. You won't be perfect, and healthy input from those you respect and those you know respect you is a good thing. But being true to yourself is even more of a good thing.

Much of art is subjective. What you think of as your best work may seem to others a disaster. Are you creating it for them or for your own desire to express yourself? Don't worry if you never sell a painting or get paid to dance. Dance, paint, sing, write to express yourself. Let the critics do what they do. They are not your problem.

Higher hurdles.

What are the obstacles to your creativity?

Lack of confidence: Of course! It happens to almost everyone on occasion. Sometimes I sit down at a piano or with a blank piece of paper and think, "Good grief! I have nothing to say. Why would anyone ever listen to me?"

Good questions! Ask them. Then do your art. Do your art for you. Much of it, perhaps, shouldn't be listened to with much seriousness. Maybe some of it should be ignored all together. But, once in a while you might just hit on something you find worthy. If no one else thinks so, so be it. If they do, it's nice frosting.

Pole vault.

What are the obstacles to your creativity?

The unhealthy state of your being? It is very difficult to pursue your creative outlet if your state of being is exhausted, stressed out, over-wrought. It is essential that you get your energy not from tension and stress but from genuine enthusiasm for the task at hand.

What can you do about it? Get your physical house in order. Exercise. I believe this as much as anything in this book, if not more. In order to be mentally and emotionally healthy, an artist—in fact, a human—must be physically healthy.

If you are serious about wanting to be in such a state of being that you can both teach and do art, get rid of a lot of unnecessary stress and tap into a fresh, new energy by being physically active. You jump that hurdle and you'll be leading the way around the track.

Don't work so hard.

Really! Take some time off to think, draw, read, ponder, play, pray.

Did you know that Americans work considerably more hours a day than residents of most other countries? If your schedule is so full that you don't have time to daydream, ponder, and pray, where will the inspiration to do art come from? People are not as impressed with workaholics as they used to be. Thank goodness. There's more to life than your profession. You are an artist, and an artist needs time for dreams and ideas to gestate.

Don't work so hard. When you get back to school in the fall, tell your principal and your school board that I told you just that.

Character counts.

You are an artist and a teacher. That's a very special combination. You don't have to be perfect at either one of them. No one is.

You also don't need to have a degree from the most revered of institutions.

Just remember that character matters more than credentials and that children are watching.

They know.

Suspend judgment.

I suppose there will come a day when we will all be judged. I, for one, can wait.

Don't be so hard on yourself. You are brighter and more accomplished than you might think. You are able to stand in front of a class of judges—we call them students—and do your thing with skill and prowess. Not many can. But you can.

And, then, don't be so hard on others. In fact, be willing to suspend judgment of yourself and others. It's not your job to judge. It is your job as both a teacher and an artist to enlighten and uplift. What a privilege!

Just do it!

Just do it. Start writing, playing, singing, painting, whatever it is you fancy to do. Just start: one word, one note, one stroke after the other, even if it's gibberish or sour. Make something. Get your art going.

Like love, art piles up. Something worthy will reveal itself if you just keep doing it.

Dream big.

When I was young and living in New York, I often attended Marble Collegiate Church down on West 29th Street. I cherished its loving ambience and listening to the messages of Norman Vincent Peale. One time I heard him say:

> *"To achieve anything significant, everyone needs a little imagination and a big dream."*

Since then, I have often thought of the notion that most of us dream too small. Most of us do not allow ourselves and our imaginations to really soar to outlandish heights.

As teachers, we pay attention to small details because we know through experience that if we take care of the small things—like classroom management, organization, courtesy, and such—the big things will follow in good stead.

But as artists we ought to dream bigger. Our imaginative art can illuminate the world and change the whole of it if we allow it to. All we need to have is a little imagination...or a lot.

Imagimotion!

Set your imagination in motion. Act on that dream today. What is one small step you could take to get yourself on the path to making your dream a reality?

If you can't think of something to do, think of something new to learn. Read about it. Study it. Listen to it. Your imagination needs stimulus and nourishment. Today, treat yourself to a new artistic experience in which you are the observer.

Seriously, when was the last time you heard a world-class symphony orchestra play live? Saw a top-notch ballet? Walked through an art gallery? Went to a poetry reading?

Plan it immediately. Your imagination is begging for it.

Who are those people?

Are the people in your life affirming?

That does not mean rubber stamps. Every idea you have is not great. (Sorry to break it to you.) But every idea is worthy of respect.

Surround yourself with people who respect you and your ideas.

Your art is precious to you. Share it with those who are worthy of your treasure, especially at this transitional stage.

Make them deserve it. But then reward them with your honest and worthy efforts.

Hero Day!

Whom do you admire the most and why? Do you really want to be more like him, her, or them? Can you learn from their examples?

Heroes are an interesting phenomenon. When I was growing up, one of my heroes was Jesse Owens. You remember him. He won four gold medals in the 1936 Summer Olympics in Berlin, much to the chagrin of one Adolf Hitler.

As a boy, I remember hearing his remarkable story and being, I think justifiably, in awe.

Years later I was singing and dancing at a banquet at which Jesse Owens was the honored guest. I remember him watching my fellow performers and me from the wings of the stage as we cavorted around the stage. As we exited, I happened to Shuffle Off to Buffalo right in front of Mr. Owens. I was as nervous and starstruck as I have ever been. Mr. Owens had a big grin on his face as he looked at my sweaty friends and me and said, "Wow! I wish I could do that!"

Imagine that. A little validation from a hero can do wonders for an artist.

As a teacher you are a hero to so many. Now who are your heroes? Let them inspire you to new heights. It's what teachers and heroes do.

Don't cry alone.

Changing your life is hard. Adjusting from your comfort zone and stepping into unpredictable new waters can be so frightening. Every so often, most artists are brought to tears by the beauty and humbling privilege of the arts and by the daunting task they have undertaken.

But remember, there is no need to ever cry alone.

Find comrades who will stick by you through joys and setbacks, who want the best for you, who encourage you to live to your full potential. Then, bawl your eyes out.

Just be sure to offer your shoulder when those fellow artists feel the weight of the privilege, too.

The secret formula that you all know.

There is a formula that most of us try to pass along to our students before they graduate and go out there on their own.

The formula is simply:

Talent + Preparation + Opportunity = Success

The talent part may in the end be overrated. But it is part of the formula.

More important, perhaps, is your preparation, so that when opportunity presents itself, you are ready. Success will be the sum of these three parts.

Honestly, does this formula work for good teaching? Certainly.

Does this formula work for artistic success?

Absolutely.

What's in your wallet?

Or more appropriately, perhaps, what's on your desk? Or, what's on your refrigerator?

Usually when I go into a home or office, I can tell a lot about my hosts by the pictures on their refrigerator or the knickknacks on the desk.

I can tell you that my desk as I write today (and every day) is surrounded by pictures of family. I also have a card that says, "There is no remedy for love but to love more." It's a Henry David Thoreau quote I love.

I have a needlepoint that my friend Lisa did for me years ago that reads, "Fate is Kind!" I always believed that, and she made the sign to remind me when perhaps I doubted or worried too much.

I have a poster from Africa that my brother gave me. It has a saying that I mentioned before:

> *"If you want to go fast travel alone.*
> *If you want to go far travel together."*

Brilliant!

I also have a yellow sticky that says "Don't forget the fish!" in my own handwriting. I left myself this note because another teacher friend of mine, Lyn from Canada, gave me a whole frozen salmon to take on the plane home with me. It was in my backpack. I didn't want to forget it. Lists are important.

What's on your desk?

How's your aim?
Are you shooting high enough?

In the nineteenth century, that great French political thinker and historian with the long name, Alexis-Charles-Henri-Maurice Clérel de Tocqueville, attributed most people's melancholy and sense of hopelessness to a "paltriness of aim."

When your short time is up on this planet, do you really want to look back and wish you had aimed higher for your students and for yourself as an artist? Abandon pettiness in your work and in your walk of life. Don't shoot for a target lower than you are capable of hitting.

Aim high.

"Paltry?" Oh, mon Dieu!

Truth more dear than certainty.

The other church that I used to attend regularly during my New York period was Riverside Church on the Upper West Side. I really loved the sermons of the great William Sloane Coffin, and the church had a good singles group.

The Rev. Coffin once said:

> "All of us tend to hold certainty dearer than truth. We want to learn only what we already know; we want to become only what we already are."

He could be pretty brutal. But he is so right. Don't you love to go to a workshop where the instructor says exactly what you already know and believe? Sure! You can nod and feel quite smug with yourself. We all do it.

But as an artist on a new path, you should take this opportunity to value truth over certainty. This is the opportunity to re-examine our core beliefs as well as our modus operandi. It would be a shame to come out the other side of this journey the same person who started it. The fact is, it would be impossible. Whew!

Prepare to work fast.

Most of my artistic endeavors are in the form of poetry, songs, or dances. And I will admit that I generally work quite quickly. The actual creation doesn't usually take that long. This book is a notable exception!

But even though I work very quickly on the art, the preparation often takes a very long time.

Get your ducks in order first: your research, your materials, your workspace, your schedule, your idea. Then the work itself can often be at a thrilling pace and make the experience exhilarating.

This is not the case for everyone.

This is the case for me and may be for you.

Wrapping up July and heading into "Auguste." Tee-hee.

Pierre-Auguste Renoir said,

> *"One must from time to time attempt things that are beyond one's capacity."*

Your fervent attempt to be both a teacher and an artist may at times seem like an undertaking that's simply beyond your capacity—beyond anyone's capacity.

That's okay. From tremendous effort, tremendous things sometimes emerge. You'll simply never know if you don't try to find out what your true capacity is. I expect it will be far greater than you ever thought possible.

215

It's your job.

It is your job to do your art—as much as it is your job to show up at 6:45 for the "before first hour choir rehearsal" or marching band. It ought to be as much of your job as going to teacher training sessions, or submitting your lesson plans to your principal, or sitting on the floor to play drums with the fifth-graders or "Itsy Bitsy Spider" with the pre-schoolers.

Doing your art is what they hired you for, even if it may not be explicitly listed that way in your contract. If the teacher of the arts doesn't demonstrate that the doing of art is a part of his or her everyday life and profession, who will? By practicing your art you are once again teaching. You just can't get out of it.

Brush your teeth.

I often try to explain to young people that I see community service as something you do as regularly and as matter-of-factly as you put on your shoes in the morning or brush your teeth. I believe that artists need to think of their art in the same way. It's a regular part of your life, not just something you luxuriate in on occasion.

If you don't brush your teeth regularly, they will decay and disappear. If you don't do your art regularly, it will decay and disappear as well. What will be left is a huge cavity that could have been prevented.

You have to do your art just as you have to do service and you have to brush your teeth.

It's not just survival!

Life ought not to be something you just want to get through. You can't survive life. You have to live it and eventually lose it. But you ought to live it while you can without focusing on the "losing it" part too much. (The end will still come. Sorry to break it to you.)

So, how will you live "it"? Hopefully you will not spend your life kicking yourself for the things you wanted to do but never, or rarely, made time for. Remember that not-so-old saying, "No one on their death bed lies there and wishes they had gone to more meetings and spent less time with family and friends."

No, the reality of a time limit is that it ought to give you courage to use the days and hours in pursuit of your real passions, not dread that it's going to get us in the end (so what difference does it make?).

This is your one chance. Do what you want to do.

Feed the son.

Do not be afraid. And even if you are…get going. Fear is not a very productive emotion. Fear and guilt can wear you down and paralyze you as nothing else can. Move forward. Don't use fear as an excuse not to move forward. Do something. You have to clean the cat box, feed the son, pick up your daughter from her lessons, feed the son, teach the private lesson, feed the son, make new reeds, tune the violins, and, oh yes, feed the son. And you have to do that which feeds your soul. Just keep moving forward. Feed the son, and feed the soul that longs to experience teaching and art. You can do it all.

Chase your rainbow.

At the end of the rainbow there might be only a casserole. I, for one, really like casseroles. You can survive on a casserole way longer than on a pot of gold.

The point is: As an artist, what you discover at any spot along your journey, or even at the end of it, may very well not be what you thought would be there. Very rarely will a blank canvas wind up looking exactly the way you thought it would when you began applying color to it, nor did the class you started teaching in the fall get exactly to where you thought it might get by the end of the semester. That's okay in both instances. It's exciting to not know exactly what's in store or what the end result will be, if there is such a thing as an end result.

Enjoy the casserole and keep chasing. There will always be another rainbow and another...well, casserole.

My friend "Q."

Once I had the rare privilege of interviewing the one and only Quincy Jones for my *Music Express Magazine*. I was more than a little starstruck. He was so generous with his time and gracious in his demeanor that he eventually put me right at ease. I said, "It's a pleasure to meet you, Mr. Jones." He said, "You don't need to call me Mr. Jones. Make it Quincy or 'Q.'" I did not say, "You can call me 'J.'" But I thought it. Anyway, he was inspirational and he had many wonderful pieces of advice to give our listeners and me.

One of Q's quips of wisdom was,

> *"If you want to know you have to go."*

We had been talking about traveling. Quincy Jones is an avid traveler for work and pleasure. But I think he meant to pass along the lesson that we all need to go in search of new experiences and knowledge if we expect to grow as teachers, artists, or just plain humans. Growth is not going to come to us. New opportunities seldom fly in the window like bluebirds or bats. You've got to go get them. They are out there. But, "If you want to know, you have to go."

———

q 2.

Here's another wise piece of advice passed along by Quincy Jones (Q to me). It's something that a mentor of his had suggested to him when Q was a young man just beginning a remarkable career that continues to take him all over the world. His mentor challenged him to "learn ten to fifteen words in as many languages as you possibly can."

Quincy said that this was the best piece of advice he ever heard and that he has tried to follow it throughout his life. Great teachers and great artists are very often intrepid travelers. As they go, they taste the food, try the experiences of different cultures, ask questions, seek to communicate and, perhaps especially, try to understand. Ten to fifteen words don't seem like very many. But start a list such as love, peace, joy, honor, courage, compassion, passion, tolerance, respect, and "where's the toilet," and you'll do all right about anywhere.

John Williams.

Since I'm shamelessly dropping names, I'll let slip one more interview I had the honor of conducting. It was with the great maestro and legendary composer John Williams. Think of nearly every iconic American movie with music in the past 35 years and you can probably guess that the man behind the music was the incomparable John Williams. (*E.T.*, *Jaws*, *Star Wars*, the first three Harry Potter movies, *Raiders of the Lost Ark*, and on and on.) Nicest man you'll ever meet, besides.

At the end of the interview I asked Mr. Williams if he had any advice for young artists who were listening to this interview. The answer, I feel, was perfect, not just for the young but also for all of us who struggle to maneuver through this labyrinth called life in pursuit of fulfillment and happiness.

"Go out and find the joy," advised the sage. "Just go find the joy."

In teaching, in your art, in your life, what could be better advice?

Who will benefit from your new priority?

What is your motive for what you want to change? Is it clear in your mind? Is it only for you or will it also help others? Is it compelling?

It seems that the people who are most successful at changing directions or broadening their pursuits are those who find some compelling reason to change course.

One compelling motive might be that your adjustment will help others as well as yourself. That is probably why you got into teaching.

So, can you define whom you can help through your art? Will you learn from it? Be motivated by it? Heal from it? Understand from it? If you can put some answers next to those questions, you might find the fortitude to answer the call.

The attention your gift deserves.

Can you identify what is absolutely the most important thing in life to you? Is that not where you want to target your creative abilities, or at least a portion of them?

Maybe you have different tiers of answers. Your relationship with God might be at the top of the list. It's hard to argue with that. But there is still plenty of room for family, friends, nature, profession, and your art on the next tier. Look at your list and examine what you think might be getting shortchanged. If your art is among the things being short-changed but you truly think of it as a priority, then you know something has to change.

You have a gift. It is your responsibility to explore that gift just as it is your responsibility to teach, parent, garden, and even pray. Where do you suppose that gift came from?

Make sure you show your gratitude by giving that gift the attention it deserves.

Resist being too cynical.

As I was reading a magazine the other day, I saw a contest in which people are supposed to send in a caption that best describes a certain photo. Most of the time, the winners try to be funny, and sometimes they succeed. There are a lot of clever people in the world. But on this occasion it seemed to me that all of the submitted captions were either extremely negative or, at the very least, quite cynical. I thought, "Have we become a nation of sourpusses?"

As a teacher and as an artist, I encourage you to resist the urge to be a sourpussed cynic. In some schools one of the best ways to do this is to stay out of the teachers lounge. But whatever it takes, surround yourself with positive people who still see the world as something to celebrate as they teach but also as they paint, write, sing, dance, and play.

Perambulate.

Go for a walk. I say that a lot. I do it a lot. The people I know who seem the most satisfied with their lives are mostly walkers. Walking clears your mind and makes room for fresh and positive ideas that are revealed in the rhythms and melodies of perambulation. Gee! That's a word you just don't use that much.

Go out and perambulate and let those rhythms and melodies sort out the song that's playing in your heart.

You're you.

Resist the urge to constantly compare yourself with others. This is not to say you cannot learn from the examples of others in the same way you are an example to your students in the classroom. Just don't get caught up in the treadmill of "They seem to have it all," "How come they aren't lost like I am," or even "I wish they were as unhappy as me."

Better to remember that you are in charge of your own happiness, your own path, your own success or failure. You are valuable as a teacher and as an artist. You are on your own schedule. You can change it if you'd like. It doesn't take bringing anybody down to lift you up. You can get there on your own. You're you.

I'm stuck in here!!

On my desk at home sits a very funny toy that someone gave me. Sometimes I move it so another family member will find it and get a chuckle out of it as I do. It's a plastic barrel about as big as your fist. It looks like one that you might ride over Niagara Falls or age some wine in. But it's a toy. Small. Yet, when you turn it over, from inside of it you hear a voice shouting, "Hey! You! Get me out of here! Hey you! I'm stuck in here!!"

I laugh every time and I've heard it hundreds of times. Do you ever feel that way? As if you're stuck in a barrel and no one is hearing your cries? No one is coming to let you out?

Well, you're not stuck. You can do the next leg of life differently. Come out of the barrel and be the person you want to be. It may shock some people the first time you say "no." Or, "I feel this way, not that." But they'll live. You'll survive and just might thrive.

The recipe of success.

Are you like me? I hate reading or doing tutorials either from a book or on the computer. I would much rather just flounder around, wasting loads of time trying to figure things out that the tutorial could have shown me in minutes.

Then, when out of complete frustration I do the tutorial, I often think, "Why didn't I just do that in the first place? This is a piece of cake!"

Most of us would not cook a fancy meal without looking at the recipe. Somebody already did the floundering for us and came up with the best way to cook or bake something. Likewise, in many aspects of our life the recipe has already been written. We don't have to reinvent it.

Check the recipes of other creative people, especially other creative teachers, and examine how they manage to do both. We can learn from those who trod this path before us.

Today, I vow to use a tutorial. Not always. I know me. But once in a while, at least.

———

Stretch and doubt.

If you believe that there is more to being a human than just your physical self, then you have to get outside of that physical self to discover it. Stretch your limits in how you approach your work, view your colleagues, question your preconceptions, tap into your new-found or once-abandoned creativity.

Have the courage to not be confident of all of life's answers. Have some doubt. It keeps you honest.

Make something.

Has it been a while since you made something? Concretely expressed your creativity with a project? It's hard to squeeze it into your busy life. But today I suggest you just do or make a little something. Something you can "fit in." You might write a verse of a poem or a refrain of a song. You might paint something or make up a dance combination you never did before. Sometimes you just have to open the spigot a bit and let the waters of creativity drip, drip, drip.

Then add another little something and another until that old creative self starts to reveal itself at last, or again, like a running faucet or a thawed pipe.

A challenging notion.

Artistic endeavors bear responsibility. I believe that art matters, that art has intrinsic power and that with that power comes a demand for accountability. I believe that art can affect the world we live in.

Therefore, I also believe that artists have a responsibility to do their art with the greater good in mind. Don't get me wrong; I am not at all suggesting that art should never be daring, frightening, revealing, even offensive if the artistic notion is to enlighten the consumer of that work. But as artists we need to be in touch with the influence we ought to wield knowingly. As teachers this is doubly so.

"Together we are better."

My friend and colleague Emily Crocker and I once wrote a song for kids to sing with that simple title, "Together We Are Better." Later, when I ran for the U.S. Congress, I used that same slogan as my campaign's rallying cry. Obviously, it didn't "rally" quite enough, but I still believe it's a good thought, and I have a garage full of campaign signs that say the same.

As you move forward into this next artistic chapter of your life, you needn't go it alone. In fact, for most artists the networking they do with other artists is an essential part of their own journey, much as teachers network with their peers to hone and tone their approach to their profession.

Seek out like-minded or even polar-opposite artist types and glean from them how they make an artistic life work in the context of their own particular set of life's circumstances. They may not all be teachers. But everybody has real life to balance even if his or her artistic life seems very well established. Then be willing to share your trade secrets if they are interested. It's challenging enough to be a teacher who is also trying to be an artist in this world. You need not fight every windmill alone.

Sometimes the windmills will win.

Yesterday I ended my epistle with the bold statement that "You need not fight every windmill alone." This is true. You have colleagues, family, and friends to help you along the way. However, today I will go on to suggest in my most Don Quixote-like style that sometimes the windmills will win. Sometimes things will not go your way.

As teachers we learn that during these times we must persevere. As artists we can do no less. There will always be another windmill twirling its sails to slow your stride. Yet, we battle onward, because we know that art is important and that the world needs dreamers like Don Quixote and all of us—teachers and artists.

Three's a cord.

Another word about cooperation and working together. In the Bible it says:

> Though one may be overpowered, two can defend themselves.
> A cord of three strands is not quickly broken.
> —*Ecclesiastes 4:12 (New International Version)*

Whether you are a believer or not, there is absolute truth in the notion that if enough people of like mind and spirit get together to support each other, very little can stop us. This is true for teachers and it is equally real for artists. I believe this is especially true if your cause is as noble as the combined profession of teacher/artist.

Amen.

Mind games.

I recently read that doing crossword puzzles won't make you smarter: It will just make you better at doing crossword puzzles. Dang! This is very disturbing to me because I love doing crossword puzzles and I actually thought they were going to keep my brain from completely atrophying before I finished middle age.

However, I'm quite certain that activities like doing crossword puzzles or sudoku can't hurt, and some studies seem to contradict the above statement completely. I'm going with it.

Certainly, there is merit in keeping your brain active by engaging in activities like reading, playing bridge, and so on. I'm not sure if slot machines count, but do keep your mind active by exercising it regularly. It can't hurt and it might just help. I am positive that being active in the arts can keep one spiritually young if nothing else. That's worth the effort.

Be independent.

This may sound contradictory after all my ranting about working together. And I still believe that working through the process together is better than always trying to go it alone. But an artist will ultimately have to be independent.

Productive, and independent.

You have to do the art. If you never produce anything you will never be independent. Produce something and free yourself.

Rabbits!

John Steinbeck once said:

> *"Ideas are like rabbits. You get a couple and learn how to handle them, and pretty soon you have a dozen."*

It is true, and brainstorming your ideas ought to be one of the most rewarding aspects of being an artist, whether that brainstorming is done on our own or with other artists.

One good idea so often spawns many more. Not all of them will be good, but all of them are important to the winnowing work you have ahead of you.

The old adage that "there are no bad ideas" is essentially true. But if you want to be productive, you need to learn how to manage all of those ideas or you're going to have rabbits everywhere! And that's not pretty.

Can you see it?

School is probably about to start again for many of you.

One school year on the first day of music appreciation class, Professor Mertens explained to his class of new college students the difference between an ophthalmologist and an artist. I liked it.

Both the ophthalmologist and the artist want us to see something, Mertens suggested. An ophthalmologist is a person who helps us see something more clearly, while an artist manipulates our perception in such a way as to cause us to see something—his or her art—quite differently. The artist/musician wants us to see or hear something the way that artist wants us to see or hear it. This perception might be quite different from what we might have first seen or heard without the help of that artist's manipulation.

As a teacher, the most powerful tool at your disposal may very well be your art and the work of other artists you love, admire, and allow to manipulate you. From an ophthalmologist you might get better vision. From an artist you might get a better Vision.

Re-creative artists.

Another professor, by the name of Mac Huff Jr., speaks of our role as "re-creative artists." In other words, especially as musicians, we often play the music that was actually created by another composer. They made it up and in many cases wrote it down. They do their best to give us as much direction as possible to help us re-create their vision. We do our best to re-create their ideas. But that re-creation can never be exactly the same as the original artist had in mind.

That's what makes art, even re-creative art, so dynamic and rewarding. Just because you are reading someone else's notes and directions off the page, or imitating what you have heard before, that action does not belittle your invaluable contribution to this particular work of art. Re-creation is an act of art, and every day you make music you are re-creating.

Two ways to be creative.

Here's a profound idea for every scholar/teacher/artist to consider. One Warren Bennis, the founding chairman of the Leadership Institute at the University of Southern California, suggested the thought. I saw it on a fundraising card.

He suggests:

> *"There are two ways of being creative. One can sing and dance. Or one can create an environment in which singers and dancers flourish."*

I suggest that as teacher/artists we are in a unique position to flourish creatively in both roles. We can, of course, sing and dance (or paint or write or play). This is the creative outlet we chose to pursue so many years ago. Or in some cases, I dare say, it chose us. But we also have the unique opportunity to spend another part of our lives creating that environment in which, largely because of our efforts, other creative beings have the opportunity to flourish. We are creators and creators once removed.

I think I'll write a check.

9/3/9

Live long and prosper.

The *Los Angeles Times* (yes, there are still some newspapers in the world, thin though they have become) ran a story of a remarkable artist who at the age of 93 is still producing art in his chosen medium. As he was quoted in the paper, "I see every day as another opportunity to create."

I believe that many artists live long, fulfilling lives as long as there is a burning desire in their hearts and souls to get up every day and make something. As long as we have a yearning to do so, we need not fear old age, assisted living, or irrelevance.

Can you change your mind?

George Bernard Shaw said, "Progress is impossible without change; and those who cannot change their minds cannot change anything."

He won a Nobel Prize for Literature. He knew what he was talking about.

You graduated from college both an artist and a brand-new teacher. You had a passion for both art and teaching. But being a teacher consumed all of your time and, by the way, paid the rent. Now as you mature, things change. You have different priorities and different needs. You want time to be an artist as well as a teacher.

The good news is that you also have more experience, at least in the teaching part of your profession. You can change your mind and your routine to reflect that experience and spend more time on that which you have neglected as you perfected your teaching chops. By now, you know what you are doing in the classroom. Not to say you could or should do it in your sleep, but you can handle more the more experience you have. If earlier you decided to dedicate yourself fully to your teaching, bravo. But, you can do both and…

You can change your mind.

It's a drag!

The middle school student walks into the classroom in complete tears; who knows why? Does he/she even know why? Somebody said something unkind to him, or just looked at her in that way that only a middle schooler can. His mother embarrassed him, his father even worse. She didn't make the team. His best friend dumped him for another. The list could go on and on. You try to convince the students that "it's a drag, but not a catastrophe." They don't buy it? Someday they will.

You walk into classroom for the fourth year of teaching or the fortieth. You wonder where the years went. You can hardly imagine how you went from being a burgeoning artist to a career teacher with nodes on your vocal cords and Boomwhackers under your desk. Your orchestra embarrassed you at the concert last night. You are spending more time at school than with your family; and don't even mention your art. The list could go on and on.

*See top paragraph for your own advice. In your mind you know that today might be "a drag, but it is not a catastrophe." Fortunately, you are not a middle schooler and you know that you can make the changes necessary to put balance and art back into your life.

And you will begin by making art with that which sits there in front of you. Your orchestra or band or choir or class. Your baton, pen, or paintbrush.

Don't buy it? Someday you will.

This is it!

How many different ways and with how many meanings can you say the phrase "This is it?"

You can say it with the emphasis on the last word and lilt up as if you are truly asking a question: "This is it?" If you do this with a shrug and a look of disbelief—if not downright disgust in your voice—you will send the message that you obviously had higher expectations.

If you say it slowly and forthrightly and emphasize the second word, as in "This is it," you will sound as though you have confidence, such as when you are lost, don't want to ask directions, and feign confidence. If you emphasize the first word and pump your fists, you will instill confidence even if those around you have doubts.

Might I suggest that as you examine your life as teacher/artist or artist/teacher you try to give each part of your "self" equal emphasis? You are artist. You are teacher. The amount of time you spend on one or the other on any given day does not give that part of you any more credence than the other in the long run. Yes, at times in your life you may act more the teacher/artist and at other times more the artist/teacher. But over the span of your lifelong efforts in both arenas, if you make the conscious effort to nurture both, you will honestly be able to look in the mirror and see artist/teacher. When you do, I encourage you to speak three words out loud with no question marks and equal emphasis: "This is it!"

—— 2/3/07 ——

"I love you!"

How many ways can you say "I love you"?

"I love you." In a whisper so that only one other person can hear it in one ear.

"I LOOOVE YOU!" Shouted from a mountaintop when you want the world to know.

"I love you?" With the emphasis on "you" and a question mark as if you're not quite sure.

"I love you?" With a sneer to rip the heart out of a wannabe lover.

"I love you." With a pleading that yearns for a response.

"I love you." Out loud with no question marks and equal emphasis on each word, into a mirror even when the struggle is hard and you find yourself so easy to disdain.

⎯⎯∘⟨⟩⟨⟩∘⎯⎯

Retirement? What the...

I am sometimes asked, and it seems a lot more often lately (hmmm…): "When are you going to retire?" or "What are your plans for retirement?"

Two questions, two answers: "Never" and "I have none."

Being an artist is not merely a profession that you do for a number of years and then abandon for golf and RV-ing—even though I look forward to some of that, too.

Being an artist is more a way of life. And good or bad, there simply is no end to it. So, teacher/artists, your day will come. In fact, it's here.

"Knock, knock, knockin' on heaven's door."

What vivid imagery in Bob Dylan's song! I imagine that when I meet my Maker I will pray the fervent prayer of every artist:

"Dear God, Not now! I've got a show to do!"

Or

"I've got an idea for a book, a painting, a song, a dance. Give me one more hour, a wefl, or at least just a minute."

Artists always have something up their sleeves or in the back of the mind that they want to create. Don't worry about running out of time or ideas. Just do your art whenever you can and keep a long list going of artistic ideas you are passionate about creating. You'll get a chance and it will keep you young…well, at least alive!

Teaching: the greatest profession.

As you struggle to put new emphasis on your life as an artist, it is important not to belittle the important work of your other chosen profession, that of a teacher. Others may do that for you, but it is inexcusable. There can be no finer profession. When you choose it you choose to walk the same path as the greatest figures in human history: Buddha, Mohammed, Jesus.

Both as artists and as teachers, it is essential to value your work—not just the outcome, but also the day-to-day, year-to-year experience of it. One path is not more valuable than the other, but our respect for the road we're on is what will make it fulfilling for us.

Expectations.

In teaching, it often seems the greater our expectations, the higher our level of motivation. This goes for both the teachers and the students on the receiving end of those expectations.

When asked who their favorite teacher was, most students will not name the teacher who was the easiest or necessarily the most "fun." Just the opposite, in fact: Students often name the teacher who expected the very most from them and, consequently, drew out the most.

As an artist we must have high expectations of ourselves just as we do of our teacher selves. The higher we set our artistic goals, the higher our level of motivation to achieve them. When we make our artistic endeavors a high priority, we will find a way to go after them.

<hr>

*You can't keep a
good teacher/artist down.*

Fall seven times, stand up eight.
—Japanese proverb

Where do you work?

It is important to make your environment conducive to being creative. But that could mean something different for every person. For a painter, loud and blaring music and a room full of light might be the perfect atmosphere to let the paint fly. For a dancer or a choreographer, a room full of mirrors and plenty of open space could be essential.

For me, when I write, I know that I cannot have music or the radio playing. I listen to it too closely. I'm not good at background music. To be free to concentrate on my own creativity I need to have my mind and space free of other people's input. I need light. I like to look up from the computer on occasion and know whether it's day or night.

I cannot have a chocolate chip cookie within walking distance because I will fixate on it until I eat it and cannot focus on my creative task at hand. "Just eat it and move on" is my general modus operandi. I need to sit up at a desk rather than recline in an easy chair or on the couch or floor. (I love that Stephen Sondheim claims to work best while lying on the couch. He says it's because it's easier to take a nap. Hey! Who can argue with those results?)

Examine your workspace and decide what you can change so it is more conducive to your creative efforts. What can you get rid of? What can you add? What can you eat just to get it out of the way?

—2/3/3—

Make time.

It is very important to make time to be creative—specific time. Carve out minutes or hours in your day or week that are specifically designated as your creative time in your freshly established creative space. (See September 7th.)

You do this for meals, exercise, and meditation, and for all of the needs of the other people in your life. Now, you need to make sure that you take care of your creative needs in a planned and productive way.

I am an early-morning person. At least I am early-morning when it comes to doing my best creative work. Those fuzzy morning hours when many people walk around in a fog are when I seem to be churning with ideas. This is when I try to do the bulk of my writing or creating. You may be a night person or realistically a teacher who has time for your own creative endeavors from 6 to 8 on Saturday morning. That's okay. Recognize it and protect it.

If you can't imagine how you will squeeze in another thing on your schedule, especially something as esoteric or abstract as "creative time," look for something you can replace. You NEED this time as an artist, in order to maintain your effectiveness as teacher/parent/partner/… human. You owe it to your students/offspring/spouse and humanity to commit to dedicated time for you, the creative artist.

Get out.

Now that I have just convinced you how important it is to have a regular workspace in which to pursue your art, I'll go another direction and encourage you to try doing your work someplace different once in a while. I am lucky to live close to a fairly decent public library. Sometimes I will go there to work even though I have nothing particular that I need to research and have a perfectly decent workspace at home that I have made my own. Yet, I find that when I go to the library I will notice something or someone that will pique my imagination and stir up a new idea, or I'll notice a nuance that will send me in a fresh creative direction. To be honest, I don't do it very often. The time it takes me to get there and back sometimes feels like too much of a sacrifice of that limited resource. But, whenever I actually do go, I find myself thinking, "I should do this more often."

No need to force it, but if you feel even the slightest need for new stimulus, if you are hitting a block or just need a change of pace, take a break from your routine and do your work somewhere else: the library, a local coffee shop, the park, a church, a tavern, or even a coin laundry.

What do you love?

Have you ever asked yourself what it is you love the most about teaching? Is it the children, or older students if you teach that level? Is it the capable and educated colleagues with whom you get to spend your coffee breaks? Is it the sense of higher calling you get from knowing that you are touching the future by helping to shape those who will inhabit it? Is it the schedule? You share the same holidays with your children and so on. Is it the fact that the teachers hold a revered position in most communities? No matter what the media tell you, this is true. People admire teachers. Most teachers deserve to be admired. What is it you just love about it? (If you can't think of anything, you might need to read a different book.) But most likely there is much you genuinely love about it when you have a second to ponder it.

So then, what is it you love about your art? What is it in your creative, artistic experience that you value the most? Perhaps you have neglected it for a while because of the incredible time and energy it takes to do your other love (teaching) well. But if you can define even one element of what it is you love about your artistic efforts, I challenge you to focus on that element and, starting today, go after it. Go after that which you love.

Get innocent.

I, for one, do not want to have a day of the year where forever and ever we are reminded of the terrible events that happened one sad September 11th out of two thousand. But in this life, it is hard to think of this date and not wonder if it is a day that will indeed be remembered as the day the USA as a country and we as individuals lost our innocence forever.

Artist/teachers, perhaps the best thought we can wrap our minds around for today is to try to regain some of the innocence that was stolen from us. Perhaps today we should try to be more childlike in our approach to our art, our teaching, and our lives. Perhaps today we can concentrate on removing the adult-manufactured blocks that hinder us in our creativity. Will my work be any good? Will I make a fool of myself? Will I be able to pay the rent if I take time to do this?

"The sea is so wide and our boats are so small." But we sail on and it will be beautiful.

Dare to begin.

It's a new day. The day to begin. Do you dare? Sometimes just getting started is the hardest thing. But this is the day. We are children again. Put one foot in front of the other. One note on a piece of staff paper. One word onto the blank page. One brushstroke. One dance step. Then another and another and another. Do not be afraid to begin. You'll need even more courage to end. But today we start and perhaps again tomorrow and tomorrow and tomorrow.

How about a poem? Here's one I wrote with my friend Roger Emerson.

A New Beginning

Dawn! A New Day! A fresh start! It's morning.
Light! The first light. A young world adorning.

Fueled by a heavenly spark; led by one beacon of hope.
Moving away from the dark to the light.

A new beginning will start today.
A chance to change and learn and know a better way.
A new beginning will start with me.
We'll find a way each day to change our destiny.
A dream that everyone can share and see the light from anywhere.
A new beginning starts today.

Stars! A Bright Star. A new dream revealing.
Life! A young life. A new hope of healing.

No one is ever alone. Nothing is ever the same.
Together we'll start moving on and on and on and on and on.

Dawn! A new day! A fresh start!
Good morning!

A better poem.

Okay, perhaps not exactly a poem, but my favorite Bible verses. Whether or not you put a lot of stake in the Bible, I suggest that as you re-examine how you will adjust your life to accommodate both your teacher and artistic selves, you keep this Corinthians passage in mind. It takes the guesswork out of how we approach each day as teacher and as artist.

> *"Love is patient, love is kind. It does not envy, it does not boast, it is not proud. It is not rude, it is not self-sefling, it is not easily angered, it keeps no record of wrongs. Love does not delight in evil but rejoices in the truth. It always protects, always trusts, always hopes, always perseveres. Love never fails."*
>
> —*1 Corinthians 13:4-7 (NIV)*

Now go through this beautiful verse and replace the word "love" with the word "teaching."

Do the same with the word "art."

That ought to get you through until tomorrow. Let's approach our teaching, our art, and indeed our love in such a fashion.

Is it worth it?

There's a song in you—or a book or a painting, or a dance or a poem—and it wants to live outside of you. The world and you both win when you express it.

Is your artistic dream worth the effort? Yes. But there may be times when you truly wonder. This doubt is not unique to you. But let me suggest that your art was something you were born to do.

Not every artistic effort needs to be shared with the world. Perhaps it is a good day to ask yourself why you feel you need to do your art. Is it to get attention from the rest of the world? Legitimate. Art can often get a person a lot of attention. Is it to express some idea or emotion that you feel a desire to share with someone in particular or with the world in general? Is it to let off steam? Show joy? Make money?

Also ask yourself about the sacrifice it will be for you and the other people in your life if you more aggressively give your artistic self the leeway to flourish. What will it cost in time? In treasure? In emotional rent?

Keep this all in mind. Then read the first two sentences of this day's missive again. Is it worth it? You bet it is. To you and all who care about you.

———

Quote for the day from someone way smarter than most.

Here is a quote so genius that it is often attributed to Albert Einstein. Other stories say Einstein chalked it on his blackboard at Princeton and gave Sir George Pickering the credit. But it appears to have first been published in William Bruce Cameron's 1963 book *Informal Sociology: A Casual Introduction to Sociological Thinking*. Whoever said it first—Albert, Sir George, William, or someone else—it's an important idea worth remembering in our quest to prioritize as we re-engage The Artist Within.

> "Not everything that can be counted counts, and not everything that counts can be counted."

So what counts?

In our magazine, *John Jacobson's Music Express,* we wrote a little show for children to perform called *Be a Star.* Each act is about being a different kind of star in the music field. In one act they sing about being a country star. The next act, a Broadway star, a movie star, and so on. The moral of the musical, and we always try to have one, came in the seventh and final act. (Of course! You can't give it all away up top!) In this final scene and song the children discover that being the very best you is the surest way to becoming a star that will shine for a lifetime. They sing:

> It's not about the Money!
> It's not about the fame.
> Not about seeing lights around your name.
> Believe in yourself and just be who you are.
> Just do your best and you will be a star!

Hey! It didn't win a Tony, but the message is a good one for children and adults alike.

Why are you doing what you are doing? Why are you interested in changing your life to give more attention to the artist who lives in you? If it's just for money, fame, and lights around your name, you will most certainly be disappointed. Those are things you might be able to count. But, do they?

Identify your passion.

You can hardly expect to pursue your passion if you don't know what it is! So the first goal might be to try to identify it as specifically as possible. You might, of course, discover that in many areas of your life you already pursuing it. (Yes, teaching might indeed be your great passion.) But today you can realize that you can have more than one. You have a passion for teaching, but you also have a passion for your family, your spiritual life, chocolate…many things.

But what is it that you are passionate about that you feel you are not being given or grabbing the opportunity to fulfill? I can't give you an answer. But I have learned that without great passion very few things happen that really elevate our human experience. Great artists have always been perhaps the most passionate people. If you are going to change your very life you certainly want to do it for something you care a great deal about.

> What do you want to say with your art?
> Do you want or need an audience? Who is it?
> What makes your pulse race as you consider it?
> What exhilarates you about whatever you feel so much passion for?
> What frightens you about it?

You won't die from pursuing your true passion, but something in you might die if you don't.

What's bugging you?

What irritates you the most in other people? It's a good question to ask yourself. Maybe you have a list a mile long. I hope not. Life's too short to be so easily irritated. As you go over that list, may I suggest that you look at those irritations and use them to try to better understand yourself?

Why does it bother you that this person always seems to get his way but never seems to pull his weight?

Why does it bother you that this person complains incessantly about how unhappy she is in her life but never does anything about it?

Why are you annoyed that a colleague uses the same lessons twenty years in a row, never goes to a conference, and complains about the students, the administration, the parents, the union, the cooks?

Ask yourself what irritates you about others, and then take a moment to look in the mirror and ask yourself what you can learn from that irritation. This is not to say that you might see yourself doing those same things (although you might), but it may enlighten you as to what kind of person you are. What kind of person you don't want to be. What kind of artist you do want to be.

Stop dreaming!

Somehow the admonition to "Stop dreaming!" seems in conflict with the overall goal or tenor of this book, which is to help you the reader rediscover the artist that is inside you and pursue your artistic dreams. However, this is indeed the exact point.

Dreams are important. But in order to make them come true, you eventually have to wake up! Wake up to the realities that shape your life and recognize the concrete steps that you must take to make those dreams come true. Change your schedule. Change your habits. Change your location. Take a workshop. Go someplace new, keep a journal, meet new people, collaborate with other artists, and so on. Keep the dream alive by waking up and taking some substantive steps toward its realization.

Sisters! Sisters!

September 20th is my wonderful sister Judy's birthday. So I feel as though I ought to pay some homage to her today. After all, she has done so much to help me over the years, both personally and professionally. It cannot be easy being the eldest of ten children, but Judy has always done it with aplomb.

I once asked Judy to please let me know when she thought I looked just ridiculous doing what I do for a living—you know, dancing around in a double dream world, encouraging people of all ages to join me in my happy dances, and so on. Her immediate response was, "Too late!" Leave it to a big sister to hold the mirror up to you at the right time.

I realize that my wise sister was merely giving me a hard time in her way (right, Judy, right?). She knows I don't know how to do anything else so this is what I will do until they cart me off to that big choir in the sky. Make certain that you have people like my sister Judy in your life to help you see the reality and the possibility of your situation—tactfully if need be but with no holds barred when necessary. Judy was not telling me to stop what I do. She was telling me that if, after all these years, I'm going to start worrying about what others think of my artistic contributions, it's going to be a pretty disappointing ride. I know that what I do with my songs and dances is good for people. I will not let others decide on the worthiness of my art for me. Neither should you. Listen to the advice of people you respect, like your big sister perhaps. But in the end, you know.

⎯⎯⎯⎯⎯

Is it real?

When my song and dance "Planet Rock" (aka "Double Dream Hands") went viral on YouTube, part of the experience was fairly disconcerting. If you have ever looked at YouTube and read the comments that people leave about any given posting, you might very well read things that would make a sailor blush. Well, they made me blush at first, too. Then I stopped reading them.

It was difficult to read that people thought I was, well, all kinds of unflattering things. It was hard to have my artistic efforts so publicly ridiculed. Then a couple of the wisest people in my life reminded me that what I do with my songs and dances is genuine. It might look silly to some, just as watching a grown-up play peekaboo with a child in the airplane seat ahead looks a bit silly, but I dance and that grownup plays peekaboo because we know it's good for the kids. We do it because this is how we genuinely contribute something positive to the world.

As an artist, you simply cannot worry what the neighbors think or you'll never do anything. But you have to make certain that your efforts are always honest. If your artistic efforts are genuine (you'll know when they are and you'll know when they aren't), a thousand cowards criticizing your sincere efforts don't amount to anything.

The meaning of life: Let's review.

Back in January I revealed to you the meaning of life. Surely you remember. Yet, early in the academic year it seems appropriate to review. Thus, today I will reiterate to you that one-sentence definition to help guide you in all of your choices as a teacher as well as an artist.

The meaning of life is to find something meaningful to do in life.

With teaching and art you give life a double whammy of meaning.

Define success.

In order for you to feel successful as an artist and as a teacher, a good exercise might be to try to define what success is. This is personal. Your idea of success is not going to be the same as the next person's. But answer these questions and see if they help you clarify what success means to you and you alone.

1. How do you think the rest of the world defines success?
2. Does it matter to you if you appear successful to the rest of the world?
3. Who do you consider the most successful people you know? What about them makes you think they are successful? Would you like to be more like that?
4. What does success mean to you as a teacher?
5. What does success mean to you as an artist?
6. In what areas of your life have you felt the most successful?
7. In what areas of your life would you like to feel more successful?
8. What is holding you back from being successful?

Opportunity: You can't get away from it!

The amazing thing about artistic opportunity, and I would go so far as to say "opportunity" in general, is that it is everywhere! Sometimes it seems as though you can't get away from it. It just knocks and knocks and knocks!

So before it knocks you over, you ought to try to recognize this as a good thing. You haven't missed the boat (see the lessons of May about missing the boat). There is still plenty of opportunity for you to pursue your dreams.

Just because you feel as if an important opportunity has passed you by does not mean that another, perhaps even better one is staring you in the face or waiting down the line for you.

True, you maybe could have been an Olympic skater had you started earlier. Probably not—but maybe. Maybe you could have been a concert pianist, a famous opera singer, a Green Bay Packer. (That was my personal missed opportunity.) But there are plenty of new artistic opportunities for you to participate in and succeed in. These are the opportunities of today, not yesterday. Answer the door. Let the opportunities of today come in.

Define a clear purpose, Part A.

If you don't know where you are going, how will you possibly get there?

You have settled into a job you love. Teaching.

Or maybe not.

You have settled into a job. Teaching.

I expect that most of you actually do love it, or much of it. But is it everything you want? I believe in being realistic at some level when setting your goals. If you are "of an age" (okay, mine) and have never played piano, you are probably not going to be a successful and sought-after concert pianist. Sorry to break it to you, but somebody had to. That doesn't mean you shouldn't take up the piano! Just be realistic about your expectations. Lowering your sights doesn't lessen the experience. In fact, a realistic approach to reaching attainable goals can be very satisfying. It's right there within your reach. But at some level you have to know what you want in order to be satisfied.

What do you want? Ask yourself.

Define a clear purpose, Part B.

1. Make a list of your talents. Whether you're using them or not, list them.
2. Write your perfect teaching/artistic scenario.
3. What contacts could you make today to help you achieve that perfect scenario today? Who could you call to lighten your load and free up some time? Who could you ask to help you create the opportunity you seek? Do you need a loan? A day off? A new space in your home?
4. Do you want more free time or more work?
5. Answer this: What do I want?

Define a clear purpose, Part C.

I realize I'm giving lots of homework this week, but it's important.

Ask yourself these two questions:

1. "Where do you want to be in five, ten, fifteen, and twenty years?"
2. "What changes must you make personally, professionally, financially, artistically to help you get there?"

You can change your mind anytime you want. But you need to know your purpose at least for today in order to get there tomorrow and the next and the next.

Define a clear purpose, Part D.

Life is complicated, and no two of us are the same. But for the purpose of this chapter I am going to break all of humanity down into two categories:

1. People who have a plan.
2. People who have no plan.

The interesting thing I have observed is that it seems that most of the people in Group One also have the drive and motivation to put their plans into motion and make their goals and dreams realities.

I have also noticed that the people of Group Two tend to drift through life and have a very difficult time finding happiness, avoiding frustration, and enjoying security.

I suggest you join Group One.

—————

Define a clear purpose, Part C.

What drives you? People who have a plan and set specific goals for their lives seem to know what they like. They know what kind of food they like, what kind of car they want to drive, where they want to live, who they want to spend time around, and what they want to achieve. They lean forward and they get things done. I suppose you could say they are driven. They seem to have a sense of direction because they know where they are going. This doesn't mean it will always be easy for them. There may very well be disappointments along the way. But for the most part these people get at it and keep their lives in motion as opposed to treading water and stewing about what coulda, shoulda, woulda....

You want to be an artist and a teacher. Why? To what end? What does life look like when you get the balance of each that you are dreaming about? Be specific about a goal that you think would make you feel as if you took a step in the right direction. Remember, this is going to be a lifetime journey and that first step is a doozy. Are you really willing to do the work as opposed to just thinking about what life could have been? You have purpose. You have a goal, or several. You are incredibly accomplished already. No one can ever take that away from you. You are ready for the next step and it is going to be beautiful. Like art. Like dance. Like poetry. Like music.

define a clear purpose, part f.

e. e. cummings wrote in an essay:

> *To be nobody-but-yourself—in a world which is doing its best, night and day, to make you everybody else—means to fight the hardest battle which any human being can fight; and never stop fighting.*

Making a life.

Why?

Question:
Why does a person who has never ever played guitar or piano decide to take it up at fifty years of age? Why does someone who can't draw a circle with a compass decide to take up oil painting in retirement? Why study French if you have no intention of going to France?

Answer:
Because these people have come to the realization that our time on this planet is not so much about making a living as it is about making a life. Every new adventure, every new thing you study, practice, read, experience, learn—master it or not—is about enriching your personal experience here on Earth. You have one crack at it—life, that is—and every opportunity you seize to make your day-to-day, year-to-year experience more full will enhance that life and very often the lives of the people with whom you share this planet. Your efforts to continue to grow as a teacher and as an artist are profoundly legitimate. You pursue them because they make you a more fulfilled you. They help you make a life.

⌐◦ 2/1/13 ◦⌐

Learn from the world.

Travel is fatal to prejudice, bigotry, and narrow-mindedness.
—Mark Twain

I realize that October is a pretty difficult time for teachers to get away and go someplace new. But I have found that traveling in October is wonderful almost anywhere in the world. For one thing, the weather is frequently sublime. And for another, all of the children are in school, so lines at Disney World are way shorter.

I have a hard time understanding how an artist cannot also be a traveler. All of the experiences you gain and all of the new things you see, feel, taste, hear, and smell are what you will draw from as you return home to do your art. As Twain suggests, nothing will open the mind more than traveling.

When you take a group of students on a trip, it might indeed be to show them something you have been studying or to reinforce some lesson with real experience. It might be to give them another opportunity to perform for a new audience, or to hear something they may never hear in their own community. But the most valuable thing you do when you take students on a trip is opening their minds to new possibilities and helping them brush away misconceptions about other places and especially other people. It works for us adults too. You will be a better artist each time you step outside your studio and take in the world.

Got skills?

I finally broke down and did one of those tutorials on my computer. It was on how to work with iMovie. I was sort of shamed into it when I saw my nine-year-old nephew using it and creating all sorts of wonderful home movies, complete with lavish special effects. He loves to blow things up—in the movies anyway. I was amazed at how helpful this tutorial was! Do you suppose that's why Apple offers it?

Your assignment for today is to do a tutorial. Learn something new that will help you with your creative endeavors. A music program like Finale or Sibelius might be a good start because you could actually use it in your teaching. If that doesn't appeal to you today, try to spend some time learning PowerPoint, Photoshop, or, as I did, iMovie. It's really cool!

If computers are not your thing, pick up an instrument you have never played and get out the level one book. Learn something new today: It makes you feel that it's still possible to do so and gives yourself the confidence that it's not too late for this old dog.

⚹⚹⚹

Think about, comes about.

What you think about, talk about, and do something about is often what comes about. Your thoughts, words, and actions are going to move you either closer to where you want to be or further away. It is essential to take responsibility, therefore, for your words, thoughts, and deeds. Filter out those that are taking you further from your goals. Focus on thoughts, words, and actions that move you closer to the life of that artist you know lives inside of you. It needs and deserves your attention.

Got friends?

Of course you do. Surround yourself with those who love and support you. Edge away from those who encourage you to be satisfied with the status quo when you know in your heart you cannot be. This doesn't have to be militant. You know the people in your life who desire for you to be the complete individual you deserve to be. Spend more time with them. You can choose to do so. You can avoid the naysayers, not impolitely, but simply by filling your life and time with those who lift you up.

Who are you reading?

Find a book or an article today about a creative person. It is so helpful to read about other people and learn from their triumphs and their failures.

Here are a few that I have found amazingly helpful.

Look, I Made a Hat: Collected Lyrics (1981-2011) *with Attendant Comments, Amplifications, Dogmas, Harangues, Digressions, Anecdotes and Miscellany* by Stephen Sondheim

Defying Gravity: The Creative Career of Stephen Schwartz from Godspell to Wicked by Carol De Giere

Helen Keller by Margaret Davidson

Sparks of Genius: The Thirteen Tools of the World's Most Creative People by Robert S. Root-Bernstein and Michele Root-Bernstein

The Artist's Way: A Spiritual Path to Higher Creativity by Julia Cameron

Getting Things Done: The Art of Stress-Free Productivity by David Allen

Ignore Everybody: And 39 Other Keys to Creativity by Hugh McCleod

ThinkerToys: A Handbook of Creative-Thinking Techniques by Michael Michalko

Poemcrazy: Freeing Your Life with Words by Susan Woolridge

The Creative License: Giving Yourself Permission to Be the Artist You Truly Are by Danny Gregory

Wild Mind: Living the Writer's Life by Natalie Goldberg

The Creative Habit: Learn It and Use It for Life by Twyla Tharp

The War of Art: Break through the Blocks and Win Your Inner Creative Battles by Steven Pressfield

Start over.

A very good question to ask yourself is this: "If you could start over, how would you do things differently?"

This is a question a president of a corporation might ask the problem solvers in his or her company: "Here we are. We need to make progress in this particular area. Pretend we are starting from scratch. How differently we might address the issue if we were not saddled with any baggage?"

For you, that baggage might actually mean your whole life up until now. I'm not suggesting that you do start over. It's a good exercise in business to get the participants thinking more broadly and it might work for your process, too. Clear the slate and design the teacher/artist life that seems ideal for you. Feel free to think big and radically.

Are there elements of that radical thinking that may not be so radical at all? Are there elements of "starting over" you could embrace today?

Speed analysis.

Here's a creative writing exercise intended to get you thinking creatively and quickly. I think it might work to get you thinking in fresh directions about your new life as well.

Here's how it works.

Get a piece of paper or a voice recorder. Now, you have ten minutes, not a minute more, to write or record how you want to change your life to allow more time for your artist self. You don't have to be neat, write or talk in complete sentences, or even make total sense. Nobody needs to see this or hear this but you. But don't think too much. Just do it. After ten minutes, look at the salient points of your own missive. Highlight them. Summarize them in one sentence. Like getting over writer's block, sometimes you have to just slop it down to get the juices started. You can always go back and reconsider. But nothing will change if you don't get started. Invest ten minutes in yourself through this process today.

Motivate yourself.

In order to be successful you have to be able to motivate yourself. If you're looking for someone else to do it, it's probably not going to happen. At least, it's not going to happen with the regularity and consistency that you need it to.

Generally, we don't have a hard time motivating ourselves to do something that we genuinely love to do: have another cup of coffee, go out to dinner, walk in the park, or lie on the couch and watch the Green Bay Packers. Exercising, going to a dieting meeting, or weeding the garden may be another story.

You probably won't have a hard time motivating yourself to do your art. It's more difficult motivating yourself to take the practical, necessary steps that put you in a position to do it. This might include lightening your schedule, changing your sleep habits, saying "no" to one thing so that you can say "yes" to something you love. The only permission you need is from yourself. But that also means it is up to you to develop a system of self-motivation that keeps you leaning forward.

Small steps.

One of my favorite quotes of all time....

"Whatever we are like, able or disabled, rich or poor, it is not how much we do but how much love we put into the doing."

Of course, those were the words of Mother Teresa.

On another occasion she said:

"To God there is nothing small."

We should listen to Mother...Teresa.

I often have young people read these words at our America Sings festivals, which combine making music with doing service. But I think it is appropriate for our discussion here as well. The effort you put into changing your life need not be done all at once. Small steps may be more appropriate and more effective in the long run. You want to love the effort and yourself as the process unfolds. Each step you take should be done out of love for yourself and your art. Each tiny step toward your goal is not small. Besides, as every good teacher knows, it is the "getting there" that often counts more than the ultimate goal. Love the process one small step at a time.

Innovation.

This page might seem to be contradictory to the last one where I encouraged you to take small, loving steps toward your goal. I don't think it is and it's my book.

In the business world, corporate executives and business schools talk about innovation. When they do they are generally talking about taking a drastic action to create change. For example, they may decide to lay off half their work force to try to instantly become lean and mean and cause some radical change and dramatic success. In a personal world, this type of innovation might mean quitting a bad habit, such as smoking, "cold turkey." It might mean giving up all of your favorite foods at once to lose weight, or quit spending money almost entirely to get out of debt. Sometimes this kind of innovation is effective and even necessary. You have to decide what works for you.

So what is the opposite of this drastic innovation? It is a gentle, methodical approach to change that takes small, loving steps forward. First one, then another, then another—winding your way toward your goal.

One or the other might be the right choice for you. As the Taoist philosopher Lao Tzu wrote more than two thousand years ago, "A journey of a thousand miles must begin with a single step." Big or small, step forward.

Columbus Day!

Sometime around this date we generally celebrate Columbus Day. (I know it moves around. I don't know why. Because he did, I guess.)

Now, I have no idea what you think about Christopher Columbus, celebrating Columbus Day, or what he ever discovered or didn't, but one thing seems fairly indisputable to me. The example set by Christopher Columbus can teach us all a thing or two about changing the courses of our lives. Here's how.

When Christopher Columbus was doing his exploring, most of his contemporary explorer competitors were sailing far, but rarely wide. For the most part they stayed parallel to the shore and as close to safe harbor as possible as they moved along. But not Chris. Instead, he headed out to sea at a direct ninety-degree angle from the shore and directly into the unknown. I have always marveled at the optimism he must have been born with, not to mention the courage and vision.

We ought to celebrate Christopher Columbus Day, whether he first discovered America or not, simply for the example he set for all of us as we contemplate the new directions in our life.

A hundred tiny changes.

Our goal is to move closer to your goal a little bit every single day. Look for a hundred small things that you can do to move forward. Say "no" to something that is consuming too much time. Say "yes" to an opportunity you have wanted to try and have not taken the time for. When you change a hundred small things one at a time, you will be surprised how big changes happen over that time. When you make these small changes one at a time, the changes tend to last.

So small you cannot fail.

One of my music teacher friends instructs his students to practice their instruments during the commercials as they watch television at home each night. (Yes! Children watch television!) He instructs them to practice their long tones by trying to play a tone through the instrument for the entire length of a commercial. This does not seem like a lot of practice time, but it adds up, and the success they feel makes them want to try it again.

Another friend of mine, a dietitian, told me of a patient who was severely overweight. The dietitian asked her to march in front of the television for one minute every single night. This did not seem like much, or enough to make much of a difference. But the woman was game for it and gave it a try. She knew she could do one minute. The overweight woman indeed marched for one minute in front of the television each night. The success she felt encouraged her to extend that minute. Over time, it was an effective approach for her because, as she discovered, part of her weight problem was due to her fear of failure. The dietitian had given her something to do that was so small she could not fail. Her success encouraged her to go to the next level.

If you want to change your life, take a small step in which you know you cannot fail. Then another and another.

Struggle.

It's a struggle. Life can be a struggle. But the most important things are born out of struggle. Think childbirth!

The most rewarding actions are often the challenges that you recognize and live through. Yes, it's hard to make a change. But you know that going in. Anyone who has struggled and prevailed will tell you that although the "getting there" may be painful when you make it through, the rewards will be all the greater. It's called "building character" and building a life of meaning.

Embrace the power that lies within.

Do you sometimes feel that things are not in your control? Perhaps you feel that so many people think they need a piece of you that nothing is left of you for you. The feeling is real even if the facts don't necessarily line up.

Yet even if many people expect so much from you and control so much of your time and energy, there is one thing that no one can control but you: your attitude. Your positive attitude is not controlled by anyone but you. Embrace the thrill of this power, and most of the direction to all of your goals will become clear. At least you will know where to look for that direction—within.

Risky business.

Success in almost anything involves a certain amount of risk, whether you are investing money, entering into a relationship, or creating a great work of art. It is risky and downright frightening to step away from something you know you are good at and go after something of which you are not so sure. But timidity has never created much of a buzz for anyone.

The fact is, you know you are/were good at the artistic field that you chose to teach. That's why you pursued it. It's just that over the course of your teaching career you may have lost some of the confidence you once had as an artist. This is the confidence that made you go to college and choose the teaching of this art form as a career. Your chops might be a little rusty. But that talent has not gone away. That confidence may have.

What would you say to your student who may have a proclivity toward one art form or another? You would say: "You can do it. Follow your heart. Prepare yourself through training and thoughtful, step-by-step progress toward your goal so that when opportunity presents itself to you, you are ready."

You should do no less yourself.

It worked for Ben.

When Ben Franklin had a difficult problem to solve or decision to make, he would take a piece of paper and draw a line down the middle of it. On one side he would write down all of the pros of a decision and on the other side all of the cons.

This process didn't make the decision for ol' Ben. But it graphically illustrated something that was only in his head, and the answer or course of action generally became more clear.

If you want to do something, change something, or be successful, you have to make decisions. Then you have to take some action. You would encourage your students to look at their lists of pros and cons and choose a course of action that would lead them closer to their goals.

Again, you should do no less yourself.

Woulda coulda shoulda.

Criticism can break down your inner spirit. So what is the opposite of criticism? Praise. Compliments. Good wishes. Respect.

It does no good to berate yourself because you have waited too long to do this or that. "Woulda, coulda, shoulda..." is a waste of energy and takes you down.

Give yourself a break and concentrate on all of the good things you have accomplished—all the lives you have nourished and changed because of the choices you have made so far. You have made the world a better place for everyone in it.

Now you can use the good energy that you deserve to make the next decision and take the next step toward reigniting your artistic fire. Don't worry: Someone will remind you when you've gone too far in your self-praise. But for now, concentrate on the good you in your past and the good you going forward.

Reach out!

Now that you are feeling so good about yourself, I want to remind you that it is perfectly all right, in fact essential, to regularly reach out to others and allow them to help you. These might be friends, family, colleagues, or new acquaintances. Try not to let ego or insecurity keep you from utilizing this valuable asset in your life.

For many problems there are support groups in almost any community. Twelve-step programs or healing circles work for a lot of people. You may or may not need that, but perhaps you could get one or two other people who you sense are dealing with the same or similar issues as you. Another teacher of the arts would seem a perfect choice. Gather these people together for coffee or a group meeting in your home or workplace. Be honest with one another about the frustrations you feel having lost touch with the artist that you believe still lives in you. You might be amazed at how your little group attracts others and how a support group like this can give you and your friends the confidence and support to move forward as individual artists. It's win-win.

Don't be sensible.

"The intelligent man finds almost everything ridiculous, the sensible man hardly anything."

—Johann Wolfgang von Goethe

I am so grateful to Goethe for that quote. When I first read it many years ago it was the first time I ever felt that there was a possibility that I might be intelligent. My friends and family quickly reminded me that I wasn't, but for a fleeting moment I reveled in my own delusions of genius.

Honestly, I have often felt that most things in the world are rather ridiculous, especially human beings and their funny, twisted ideas. Come on! Double Dream Hands?

But the most ridiculous of all human follies is the fear that if we try to make significant changes in our lives the sky will fall and all that we have accomplished so far will be for naught. In the words of another brilliant thinker, Paul Mertens, "This is fuzzy thinking."

You won't die because you take that flute out of the closet and try to play it again. You won't lose your spouse if you take up painting or poetry, or audition for the community theater. Fear of trying something new is ridiculous. Don't be sensible.

"It'll set you free!"

My friend Ruth Ann uses a phrase that I have now adopted. The phrase is simply "It'll set you free!" (She's from Texas so there is often a "ya'll!" added to the end of it, as in "It'll set you free, ya'll!" even if she's talking only to you. It's one of the many mysteries of Texas.)

Regardless, I think it's a marvelous phrase. Ruth Ann will use it when referring to a particular piece of music she thinks you ought to hear or a new dessert she wants you to try. "You should try this, ya'll! It'll set you free!"

In a more literal sense and for today's discussion, I think we should focus on what you can try that will set you free to pursue your quest as teacher/artist. Which of these could you try to help set you free?

- I will cut this from my schedule so that I can have time for that.
- I will say "no" to that so that I can say "yes" to this.
- I will not worry about the quality of my artistic endeavors yet. I will just get started.
- I'm doing this for me, knowing that a more fulfilled me makes me a better partner, mother, father, sibling, colleague, teacher, friend, and artist. Ya'll!

Relax.

What are you doing in your life to help you relax? The changes you are making should not happen under duress or stress. You are changing your life because you want to, not because of some trauma. These are decisions you are making and steps you are taking to reinvigorate your artistic self as a reasonable, experienced, accomplished adult. But you can't do it if you're all stressed out! (Sorry for the shouting. Just got a little stressed.)

Seriously, what are you doing to help yourself relax? Everyone should plan relaxation activities as a part of their routine. For you that might mean massages, yoga exercises, long walks, and so on. These are not indulgences. These are necessary for you to be in the physical and mental position to make sound, stress-free decisions about how the next chapter of your artistic life will unfold.

Today, plan one activity (lying in a hammock counts) that helps you relax, and prepare yourself joyfully for the tasks and exciting challenges that lie ahead.

Pay attention!

Pay attention to yourself as an artist by observing your choices and dwelling on your motivations regarding those choices.

Why do you react to any given situation the way you do? For instance, when people ask you to do something for them, is your immediate answer yes? No? Let me think about it?

When you say yes or no to a new artistic experience, what motivates that decision? Is it your need for attention? Is it your fear of attention? Are you looking for strokes? Are you afraid of criticism? Are you worried about making a mistake? Is the art for you? Is it public? Private?

By making a mental or actual note of your own motivations, you may be able to address how to change your actions to better promote your renewed artistic ambitions.

Pay attention, and then try a different approach to a situation you have been in many times and in which you generally behaved in a predictable pattern. You might be surprised and encouraged by an unfamiliar result.

We are all winners.

I am often asked to be a judge for music competitions. I generally say no. It's just not my thing. I've always thought that the arts ought to be one place where everyone can be a winner. Judging art always seems like apples to oranges to me.

It's important to remember that your art is your personal expression. It comes from you. It is about you. It reflects you. There's no real win-lose about it.

You are not in competition against other artists. They are expressing themselves as you are.

Even in our sports/politics/business-driven world, it seems as though we all should be reminded from time to time that we are competing with each other, not against each other. If there is to be an element of competition in the arts, this is especially true. Your success as an artist is a boon to the entire world. There are no limits to how many winners we can have in the arts: The more the merrier. You will be one of them.

Where's the love?

What is it that you love about your art? What is it in your art that you value the most? Is it the reaction you get from your audience? That's valid. Is it the actual process of making the art? It is for me. I like rehearsal. I like the way you get to do something over and over in rehearsal, trying to make it better each and every time. To me performance has always been a way to end rehearsal, so fleeting that it often feels rewarding in a much different way from rehearsal, sometimes not nearly as satisfying as a good, sweaty rehearsal. But that's just me.

Can you identify what it is you love most about your art and go after that? If you haven't given it much thought, perhaps it would be good to do so today.

—————

you!

If you're looking for someone else to do it, you're in trouble. You have to motivate yourself. Generally that will not be hard if you are pursuing something that you genuinely love. There are so many places that you can look for motivation; books, recordings, museums, the theater, a dance studio, a concert hall, a misty woods are all good places to find inspiration. But you have to be the one to get yourself there. You get the tickets. You drive yourself to the park. You sign up for the lesson. You read, listen, watch, act.

This doesn't mean you can't go to others for help or advice. This doesn't mean you can't get a support group together to encourage one another. But you have to attend the meeting. You have to seek the help, organize the group, attend the session, act.

You are not alone. But it's up to you.

—◁≡≡▷—

Expect to win.

The beautiful actress and humanitarian Audrey Hepburn is quoted as saying, "Nothing is impossible…the word itself says 'I'm possible!'"

And although French statesman Chrétien Malesherbes wrote these words in the 18th century, I think of legendary Green Bay Packers Coach Vince Lombardi when I hear them: "We would accomplish many more things if we did not think them impossible."

Others have used phrases such as "visualization." A pole-vaulter visualizes the run, the planting of the pole, the lift, and the act of going over the high bar before he actually takes off to try it. In his mind he has already seen himself hurling his body up and over. Then, in theory, he does it.

We need to visualize ourselves as artists. We need to see ourselves going through the motions of performing our art. We need to imagine ourselves making the changes in our lives that will make the pursuit of our art possible. We need to expect that we will be artists, or we cannot be artists. We expect it. We visualize it. Then we do it. We believe "I'm possible" and we make it so.

Be.

A singer has to sing.

A dancer has to dance.

A painter has to paint.

A writer has to write.

A musician has to make music,

A composer too.

You have to be what you have to be.

What shall you become?

You have spent a lifetime preparing to be and then becoming a teacher. You're good at it. You ought to be. It's been your life's work. When people look at you they think "teacher." What could be more rewarding than that?

Yet, you want more. And you should have it. You are more. And you should do it.

Try not to let yourself be held back by what you have been, or what others perceive you as. They see you as a teacher. But how do you see yourself? You can be a teacher and an artist. Don't let your past define what you will be in the future. If you see yourself as a teacher and an artist, but your experience and effort have labeled you as one or the other, you can change that experience and effort from this day forward. What you will become is not determined by what you have been. You will become an artist when you proceed as an artist.

Always a teacher.

Even if you should decide to dramatically change courses for the next chapter of your life, chances are you will never stop being a teacher. You teach. That's what you do. It's in that blood that pumps through your heart.

But teaching, like art, often pauses in interesting places. Now might be one of those interesting pauses for you. Now might be a time to reflect on the role that teaching will play in your life from this moment on. Most likely, teaching will not go away. Most likely, you don't want it to. But during this pause you might find a way to begin again with a new perspective on both your teaching and your life as an artist. You take a breath and step off the treadmill that has been your teaching life for however long. When you step back on, it might be with some variation that leaves room for you the artist as well as you the teacher. You haven't made a mistake by dedicating your life thus far to teaching, and teaching is not going away. But what will you become tomorrow after this little pause? You'll decide.

There may be more pauses in your life as a teacher and as an artist. They are all interesting.

Professional development.

Most schools have professional development days in which teachers sit in a room and behave like, well, students. Many times the purpose of these days is to try to develop as a faculty in order to more effectively serve the students in your care. I expect that sometimes these development days are very worthwhile and other times, well, not so much.

Perhaps the most effective form of professional development is personal development. All teachers have passions, hobbies, skills, and a self outside of the one that they show to their students every day. Your development of those outside-the-classroom facets of yourself is crucial to making you more effective inside the classroom.

Your development of your artistic self may, well, make you a better teacher.

Your role as artist/teacher.
or
Your role as teacher/artist.

You decide which goes first on your own résumé.

The most important role you may play as a teacher is to tap into your own artistic experiences and share them with your students. If you sincerely want them to develop personally and artistically, pursuing their passions with confidence, what better way to ensure that than to do so yourself? When you let them share in your adventure, who knows what you might unleash?

Still growing after all these years.

"Every child is an artist. The problem is how to remain an artist once he grows up."

—Pablo Picasso

You got that right, Pablo! And anyone who teaches children in the arts is acutely aware that children are capable of creating incredible art. It may not be the same art they would create as an adult, but it is as valid a reflection of their experience and interpretation as any adult's art.

How then do we keep the artist alive as the child grows up?

Perhaps that is ultimately the essential question of this book.

Anything you quit or ignore always seems harder to pick up later; participating in sports and playing a musical instrument come to mind. But it is not impossible. Ideally, the trick is to never stop. Keep the children involved in the arts right along and perhaps they will continue to express themselves artistically into adulthood.

That works for us, too. Never stop doing your art. But if you have stopped, start again. It may not come back as quickly as you wish. Your first efforts may fall way short of what you remember being able to do when you were younger. However, a child's art will not compare to what the child can do as an adult. It need not compare. The art you produce in your future need not compare to that which you produced in your past. It will be different and equally worthy.

Domo Arigato Mr. Ikemoto

"When my daughter was about seven years old, she asked me one day what I did at work. I told her I worked at the college—that my job was to teach people how to draw. She stared back at me, incredulous, and said, 'You mean they forget?'"

—Howard Ikemoto

I am a big fan of the artwork of Howard Ikemoto and an even bigger fan of the teacher Howard Ikemoto is. Mr. Ikemoto is a second-generation American Japanese who was born in Sacramento, California, in 1939. He says his first drawing was of the internment camp at Tule Lake where his family was placed during World War II. After the war he went on to elementary school, then high school and college, and eventually spent thirty-four years teaching at Cabrillo College. At one point during his years of teaching, Mr. Ikemoto took a break and lived in Japan to learn more about his family roots, but he says he learned even more while there about Japanese culture and the subtleties of their aesthetics. It affected his teaching and art forever. Since he has retired, Mr. Ikemoto has spent his life doing his art.

Notice all the things Professor/Artist Ikemoto did right: Studied other artists. Took a break from teaching and "fed" himself in another setting. Ramped up his artist side when his teaching obligations waned. Continues to teach by example every day.

We don't forget to draw. We just have to pick up the pencil again when we're ready.

―――――

Enjoy!

Teaching, creating art, experimenting, tasting new foods, listening to music old and new, going to different places and meeting different people, opening our hearts and minds to different perspectives and other people's life experiences, seizing the brass ring of opportunity when it presents itself or creating new opportunity even when it seems elusive, embracing the unknowns of tomorrow, redefining ourselves at any age in small or dramatic ways. It's all good.

Never grow up.

There is one area of life that I am fairly confident we are never sup-posed to outgrow and that is the pursuit of knowledge, truth, and beau-ty. Artists and teachers are like children in their eternal chasing of all that is meaningful, beautiful, and honest in the world. We shouldn't be concerned that we have reached this point in our lives and still don't feel that we have "figured it out." Life is a childlike journey that we travel with our childlike eyes wide open to new experiences, new ideas, new opportunities, and especially new illuminations of what we per-ceive as truth. You're not on the downward slope. Like a child, you're just getting started.

You may not be Monet.

It is easy for those of us who admire great artists to allow their greatness to intimidate us right out of pursuing art of our own. How could anyone sit down and try to write a symphony after listening to Beethoven, sing an aria after listening to Marilyn Horne, or paint a canvas after reveling in Seurat?

If you compare yourself to the greatest artists in your field, you might easily think, "I could never do that, so why bother?"

However, if you instead focus on what is it about these great artists that you truly admire, and try to incorporate that element into your own work, you may actually find inspiration in their mastery. Believe it or not, they too had artists they modeled themselves after. If you wanted to be a composer and carefully studied how Bach used counterpoint, Andrew Lloyd Webber wrote melodies, Gilbert and Sullivan came up with lyrics, and so on, you may never do any single element as well as any of them. But the work you do after accepting them as your teachers may be truly inspired by those incredible role models. That's why you bother.

Your latte or your life.

One of the biggest reasons I hear that people can't make the changes necessary for them to pursue happiness is that they can't afford it.

"I can't afford to give up my Thursday night community choir job because it pays me this much a week!" "I can't afford to take my summer off from teaching and go to classes that will help me in my artistic endeavors because I need the money that my summer job brings in."

You know.

I hear it from students all the time: "I'm broke!" Often, they seem to be telling me that over a steaming cup of $6.50 latte. (I have no idea if lattes cost $6.50. But I know they are expensive. I'm a flavor of the day guy myself.) The point is, if money is tight and that "tightness" is getting into the way of your artistic pursuits, watch every penny more closely. I'm not asking you to deny yourself everything you love. But, be aware that your choices have consequences. Is a $97 latte (They probably are not $97. But hey…they are expensive!) worth it if it means you can't afford the time to pursue your art? Don't confuse wants with needs. And don't value money more than art.

Amen.

I'm no Einstein but...

It's hard to imagine modeling yourself after someone who figured out the special theory of relativity when he was in his mid-twenties. I think at that age I was choreographing the Winnie the Pooh for President Inaugural Parade. But one area where we can all model ourselves after Albert Einstein is in his approach to his work. I have read that Einstein said the secret to his genius was in his ability to look at problems in a childlike, imaginative way. He called it "combinatory play." I think he made that word up.

I think "combinatory play" probably included a lot of doodling and daydreaming, and if it's supposed to be childlike, then it must have a lightheartedness and playfulness even if the work is very serious and the consequences are adultlike.

Can we approach our work in the same way as Einstein did? I think it is essential. Go ahead—daydream, doodle, lighten up! You know, like Einstein.

Goals and dreams.

Goals and dreams are two very different things. Both are important, and it's important to have both and know the difference.

A dream is something you desire. It is in your mind and heart and it may or may not ever come to fruition.

A goal, like a dream, is something you desire, but it's more specific. You can measure a goal, where a dream can often be immeasurable. Goals can be stepping-stones to reaching your dreams, and that's why you need to set goals if you ever want to reach your dreams. Goals help you be who you want to be. They stretch you. They boost your confidence. They give you a purpose. They give you manageable benchmarks that let you prove to yourself that you are making progress. They are satisfying.

What are your goals for the coming week? Month? Year?
What obstacles are in the way of your reaching these goals?
Who will help you reach your goals?
When you reach these goals, how will you celebrate and how will you plan the next set of goals?
Will these goals help you realize your dreams?

Goals.

I want to encourage you to share your goals. You can share your dreams, too, but begin by sharing your goals with people who can help you achieve them.

Of course, this should be a person or people that you trust and who you know want you to reach your goals. This journey need not be taken alone. In order for people to help you achieve your goals, they have to know what they are.

Your shared goals can be grand or small. Make them specific. Call on your dream team to help you achieve your goals, goals that move you ever closer to your dreams.

Be positive.

I believe so strongly in the power of positive thinking to help us survive, thrive, reach our goals, and pursue our dreams. Being positive is the best way to keep yourself motivated. Enthusiasm can be supported by exercises in positive thinking. Here are a few. Give them a try.

- Make a list of your good qualities. You don't have to share them with anyone but yourself. But do so regularly.
- Make another list of the good things you have in your life. It's not greedy to recognize the good things and lovely people you have in your life.
- Remember nice things people do or say about you. Write them down if you need to. Read them when you need a boost.
- Write down your worries. In black and white they may not seem so overwhelming. In your mind they can get blown out of proportion.
- Do something nice for someone else. It would be easy for your pursuit of your dreams to be extremely self-centered. Doing for others will keep your goals and dreams in perspective. You might even remember how good you have it, and that's a good place from which to begin your new life.

The worry hour.

A friend of mine, who shall remain nameless, recently told me that she was seeing a sleep specialist. She had a lot on her mind and the specialist was trying to help her get the rest we all need. One of the pieces of advice that the specialist offered was that she should have a worry hour every evening in which she would write down all the things that she was worried about. The idea is that once they were on paper, they would seem less daunting, more organized, and less sleep-disturbing.

If my friend ever wakes up I'll let you know if it worked.

It's not a bad idea to make a list of what scares you about the changes you are about to make in your life. What are your worries? That you will look foolish? That you will be unable to perform your art the way you used to or the way you want to? That you won't be everything to everyone?

Write them all down and then go get a good night's sleep. Obstacles such as these shouldn't stop you from pursuing your artistic dreams. You can tackle worries one at time, and if you write them down they may not seem as daunting as they did when they were just in your head.

It's expensive.

Time spent not pursuing your dreams is very expensive. How much is it worth to you?

If your work is costing you your life, you must have decided that it is worth the price you are paying. That's very good.

If the cost seems too high, there is a real motivation to redirect your spending habits so that your life's seconds and minutes are consumed doing what will bring you the greatest rewards.

———————

Courage!

Do you have the courage to imagine the many possibilities for your life? Because, indeed, it does take courage to take stock and courage to make change.

And the answer is, of course you do. You walk in, mostly unafraid, every day to a classroom full of students, each full of questions, issues, possibility. You have the courage to serve as their mentor, example, motivator, disciplinarian, and so much more.

Now your challenge is to use that same courage to face the unlimited possibilities that lie ahead on your life's path. I'm not one of those who necessarily believe that because you can imagine something you can achieve it. But I do believe that it would be impossible to achieve something that you cannot even imagine.

Don't be afraid to let your imagination shoot for the stars. You are living with the spark of unlimited possibilities and you absolutely possess the courage to first imagine them and then chase them down.

Hard work vs. heart work.

Is your work hard for you? Is it hard on you? This does not mean that it isn't rewarding. And work can be challenging even when you love it. In fact, sometimes we love our work for the very reason that it is challenging. But it should not be hard on you, beating you up and wearing you down. If it is, something needs to change.

Most of us chose a life in the arts because it truly was our hearts' work. We loved the practice, the rehearsal, the process, and the result. We loved the role the arts played in the world. Likewise, we chose teaching because in our hearts we felt it was important and rewarding work that, aligned with our love of the arts, was the perfect combination for those who can both do and teach.

But if what started as your heart's work has somehow sunk to the drudgery of hard work, it is time to re-evaluate, refer to the November 15th missive, and muster the courage to imagine a life where we reconnect with the possibilities of our hearts. This is not to say there won't be days less rewarding than others. But if every day of work is just hard, it's time to follow your heart.

Create!

I sometimes worry that we live in a nation—and perhaps a world—made up of mostly consumers and very few creators. In fact, so much of our economy is based precisely on the fact that we all consume stuff. When we slow down our consumption, our economy suffers greatly.

Although artists are also consumers, I think most of us are drawn to the arts partly because the arts give us an opportunity to make something. This is not unlike teaching. In fact, teacher/artists are creating on both sides of the slash mark.

As you re-examine your new life that perhaps flips the artist to the other side of equation, I encourage you to engage in work that creates rather than consumes. This will be an inspiration for your students and will fulfill a need in you on your artist side that you may have ignored on your teaching side.

What are you going to make today?

—⋅⋅⋅⋅⋅—

Responsibility.

As a teacher you are rewarded or burdened with huge responsibility: the education and character development of a whole new generation, if nothing else. Unfortunately, although much is expected of you, you are often denied the power to actually tackle the responsibilities effectively.

This is why getting the arts to the forefront of your life again is essential. When you are immersed in your art, you can afford yourself a power that matches your responsibilities. You are in charge of your own artistic statement. There is a responsibility that comes with that. But you control that responsibility way more than you will ever be allowed to as a teacher. That in itself ought to be enough motivation to go after it. When all else seems to be spinning out of control, it is your art that will ground you and give you the power to meet your responsibilities.

What do you want?

What do you want? Sounds like a question a frustrated parent might ask a screaming baby, or a frustrated teenager might ask a screaming parent. WHAT DO YOU WANT...from me? From them? From your peers? From your students? Family? It's a fair question. But let us ask it more analytically, or at least more gently.

What is your objective? Can you answer that regarding yourself as an artist? What do you want to create? Because art is about creation. Likewise, as we've already discussed, creating art is about goals. Goals, creation, responsibility, objectives and, oh yes, values.

You teach with a core set of values that you embrace and hopefully reconsider on occasion. Reconsidering does not necessarily suggest making a change, but surely no one can understand every one of his or her core values...ever. "They take constant examination and reconsideration!" preaches a man sometimes known as JJ.

Now as you set new objectives for your life as artist/teacher, make one of your goals that your artistic endeavors squarely match the values you have embraced as a teacher and as a human being. It is your responsibility as an artist to do so and it will make your creations ever more honest and fulfilling.

—◁/◁/◁—

Superstar!

This morning I was working on a new song that is supposed to encourage young people to go after their dreams, be the best that they can be, take chances, be brave, be the shining star they want to be. It struck me that it is not too late for all of us to listen to the voices inside our heads and hearts and get after it; whatever "it" is for us. The song goes like this:

Superstar

Everybody has a dream.
To shine just like the sun.
As hard as it might seem
You can be the one!
Just be who you are
You've just got to try!
Always room for new stars
In the endless sky!

You're a Superstar!
You're a Superstar!
No matter what they say
Every night and every day
You are going to go far!
'Cause you're a Superstar!
You're a Superstar!
Just give it your best.
You can rise to the test.
Go be what you are!
Go be a Superstar!

Grade your own papers.

November 21st is the birthday of my dear brother Steven, who passed away a few years ago after a too short yet brave life. So I dedicate this page to him. Steve was an inspiring and demanding teacher; just ask any of his students. He went way beyond the pale in so many instances and, like so many good teachers, changed the lives of countless students in sometimes small, more often profound ways.

One of the ideas my brother passed along to his students at graduation and other times was that, in the end, they were all going to have to grade their own papers in order to really understand how they performed in life. No teacher was going to be standing over their shoulders or making red marks on their records. They would be the ones to judge their successes and failures, at least in the mortal part of their existence. As humans we need to look honestly in the rearview mirror and have a sense of how we did, and in the front mirror at how we're doing now.

So, how will you grade your paper? Did you have the courage you admonish your students to have in pursuing their dreams? Did you give life its best shot both as a teacher and as an artist? As an individual as well as a part of the community of humankind? Just because it may not have turned out the way you expected does not make for a failing grade. You will know the parts in which you deserve an A for effort and a D- for success. Perhaps you will recognize that that grade might be more valuable than the one where you got a C for effort and an A for reward. Only you will know. Only you need to know.

Step up.

A big future is laid out in front of us. Depending on your religious beliefs it may stretch forever or not very long at all. That's for you to ponder.

But the fact is, whether the future is long or short, infinite or waning, it is there for the taking. Someone is going to step up and fill the future with new ideas and experiences that make it vibrant. It could be you. You could be the one who steps up and takes the control of the future, at least your own. It cannot be more of the same. There will be new experiences, opportunities, successes, and failures, whether you admit it or not. There may also be ones that you create through your daring approach to the days ahead. Be the one who steps up and shows the world around you what it truly means to seize the day. The future is there for someone to grab hold of. It might as well be you.

With or against.

November was a busy month for birthdays in our household. Of course, in a family of ten children, almost every month was busy, especially when in-laws and grandchildren started to crowd the calendar. November 23rd is the birthday of "The Twins," my brother Kerry and sister Sherry, both teachers of the highest caliber. Kerry was born first, by minutes, so I'll give him today and dedicate tomorrow's page to Sherry. I've learned so much from both of them.

One of the many important lessons Kerry taught me was about competition—in sports and in life. Growing up in our large family, we always had some sort of competition going on. Perhaps competition is a constant in your life, too. In a speech to two competing schools sharing the same campus, my brother said this:

"It is important to remember that we don't compete against each other, we compete with each other ... especially when we compete with our brothers and sisters.

"[At our school] we don't believe in the old sayings 'Boys will be boys' and 'Girls will be girls.' No, our core values and our mission make it clear that 'Boys will be men' and 'Girls will be women.'

"[Spiritual teacher and writer] Sri Chimnoy observes, 'We compete not for the sake of defeating others, but in order to bring forward our own capacity.'"

So, I suggest you adopt this philosophy as you seize your future with a competitive fervor, realizing that your success is not heightened or lessened by the success or failure of your colleagues, family, or friends. When one of us succeeds, we all win.

You did it right.

Kerry's twin is my bright sister Sherry, less ebullient perhaps than dear Kerry, but no less wise and experienced as a teacher, a parent, a sibling, a spouse, and so much more.

"Teachers are smart." That's what Sherry reminded me. They have chosen a smart lifestyle. A lifestyle that sets a good example to the rest of society when it comes to planning ahead so that when you are ready to move on to something else you are able to do so. Sherry says:

"Saving for retirement is also something that is both a sacrifice that public employees have chosen to make and a wise social statement to all of us Americans as a way of saving the public many dollars later. These public employees will be better equipped to take care of themselves in retirement again, saving future public spending."

I'd vote for her. Why this is relevant to this journey we are on is that it reminds us that the responsible and rewarding path you chose as a teacher was also a way of setting up your future to allow you to pursue other dreams, such as your own art activity. You did a smart thing when you became a teacher. You took matters into your own hands by saving for retirement, taking less along the way so that it would last longer, planning so that you are not a burden to society or anyone else. You are free. Now, you are in a position to pursue that matter at hand.

Overburdened with talent?

We were standing around the kitchen making another monumental holiday meal. The conversation drifted to being about me and my exploits. I don't exactly know what led up to this statement, but at one point lovely Aunt June looked directly at me and with all sincerity said, "John, you are overburdened with talent!" My siblings covered their mouths and ran from the room, nieces and nephews loudly guffawed, and the chocolate soufflé collapsed. Don't ask me why.

Anyway, perhaps you feel that you were, too.

The bottom line is that the talent you were given as a musician and the training you received to develop that talent have provided you something that could be seen as a burden. But in truth you know that it is less of a burden than an opportunity. You were born to create. You know it in your heart and that is why at this point in your career you are trying to once again embrace it.

Go now and find something that reflects the beauty of human creation. Maybe it is a recording you made of yourself. Perhaps it is a poem you wrote or a painting you painted. Maybe it is not even something that you made but something that reminds you of the beauty of creating something. If you can't think of anything, go find a colorful leaf and examine what a Higher Being has created. As an artist you were born to create. You are not overburdened. That Higher Being did not give you anything you should not embrace and celebrate.

But it's scary!

Getting back in touch with your artistic, creative self can be very frightening. I personally don't believe that the fear will ever go away, even though creating art seems to require a fearlessness few of us ever really feel.

You can never count on not being afraid of the risks it takes to truly be an artist. But you can work on the sense of optimism it requires to transcend that fear and continue on your creative path.

That optimistic feeling will be easier to maintain if you put practices in place that guide your artistic endeavors and perhaps even give your life over to a Higher Authority who is your ultimate judge and support.

So first, be practical in your daily approach to your art. Do the things we already talked about, such as making regular time to create, getting rid of the clutter of your life, saying no to things, and so on. Then, or simultaneously, include in those practical steps a regular commitment to meditation, prayer, exercise, pondering, or whatever works for you to keep your artistic self optimistic and able to handle the inevitable fear.

Build.

Often, when we are teaching, it seems we are in a deconstructing mode—taking things apart so our students can understand how they work. In our artistic lives we need to do just the opposite. We need to be constructors of new creations. This takes a dramatic shift in the way we approach our art. I might even suggest it may be a more effective teaching approach in most instances.

Along with the optimism we discussed yesterday, there is a requirement to embrace practices that help you be constructive rather than destructive in your process. Build your art from the ground up so you feel you are creating as opposed to deconstructing the walls of ignorance that a teacher is often called upon to do.

> Keep a journal.
> Take a class.
> Get a voice lesson as opposed to giving one.
> Build a workplace to do your art.
> Commit to at least one artistic goal.
> Join an organization of like-minded artists.

These are the kinds of things you can do that will reconstruct the artist in you.

Be a star!

Okay, this may seem a little cheesy, but where I come from "cheesy" is a grand compliment so bear with me.

It's an exercise. Make a picture of a five-pointed star. At the tip of each point write something that reminds you of a rewarding artistic experience in your life. It would be best if each of the experiences was something that you created as opposed to simply witnessed.

Now, inside each ray leading up to that point write a few words about why that experience was so meaningful or rewarding to you then or why you now remember it as being rewarding.

Next, pick out at least one of those rays and take one concrete step toward re-creating such an experience at this stage in your life. It will not be the same experience. But we are working toward re-creating the successful feeling you had as an artist once and know you can have again. First we'll identify it, then we'll work toward making you shine. (Okay, that really was a cheesy line! So be it!)

Be a star! Step 2.

Now that you have identified a positive experience, or maybe five, can you make a list of impediments to making that vision come into fruition? It may be a little more complicated than merely "I can't sing that note anymore," "I can't leap as high," or "I have no gallery or stage to perform in."

Make a list of your life habits that are getting in the way. Some might be big and obvious (smoking, drinking too much, overeating, never exercising, and so on). Certainly, those are hurdles and should be worked on.

But let's think of hurdles that are perhaps less overtly destructive: such as you are always helping others so have no time for yourself, you are hanging out with people who belittle or couldn't care less about your dreams, or you read books or magazines, watch television shows, or obsess over the Internet and get nothing back from it.

Now write down a complete thought that starts like this:

"Today I will make my artistic self more of a priority. To do so I will......................"

In your answer, address first the more subtle issues above. I have a feeling that when you break down some of these surmountable obstacles to your creativity (spending less time on Facebook or in front of the TV, avoiding or confronting a negative or disrespectful friend or colleague, etc.), those big issues that seem impossible to change may not seem so daunting after all.

It's a marathon.

We are closing out November and heading into the last month of the year. No matter how we plan, who really knows what might be in store? No doubt we'll run from one obligation to the next like sprinters in the ancient Olympics—hopefully mostly clothed!

Alas, it is easy to see your life and career as a series of such sprints. We mark off the tasks and measure our progress by short spurts of energy and accomplishments or even failures. We view life as something pieced together by these individual events. But as we head into this final month I'd like to suggest that we instead look at our lives, and especially our careers as teachers, not so much as a series of sprint races but as a lifelong marathon.

Certainly, there will be milestones along the way: peaks and valleys that make life seem like a patchwork or a series of short spurts of energy. But I suggest trying to remember that the big picture is in the long run. Often progress will be slow and arduous; other times fast and exhilarating. But as we look back at the track behind us I hope we will be able to see a road well-traveled and a path worn mostly with beautiful memories of more success than failure, more highs than lows, more wins than losses, more strength than weakness.

Certainly we encourage our students to recognize that sometimes life is hard. Come on! Music Theory 101! But their lives and yours will not be judged by this little triumph or this big mistake. It will instead be judged by the total result of this marathon we call life in which, perhaps ultimately, you are the only contestant in your particular race. You can't lose. All you've got to do is keep your eye on the prize: a long life filled with best efforts, noble causes, a few stumbles—but even more triumphs.

Your life is a marathon, and with every stride along the way, you will make the world a more beautiful and harmonious place to be. For you, indeed, are a teacher of art.

Three little words.

I often end my workshops/classes by acknowledging that my life's philosophy can pretty much be summed up in three-word phrases. You are probably thinking, "Why then did you wait to tell us this until December?" I don't know. See, three words.

"I don't know" isn't my life's philosophy, okay? And technically it's a stretch of the three-word rule, but you can say a lot in three words. So I now intend to end the year with the pithy little phrases that guide my life, in the hopes that maybe they will help guide you, too.

"I don't know" may not be the best one to start with, but realizing that you don't know isn't a bad place to start. Admitting that you don't know everything might open you up to new ideas and new directions. Beware of anyone who pretends to always know.

As you approach this next chapter in your life, you can't know exactly what will transpire. You certainly can't know how it will all turn out in the end. Not knowing should be thrilling, not frightening. As long as you listen twice as much as you talk and are willing to approach your demons no matter who or what they are, what you don't know now is not going to be the end of you. The trick is to prepare yourself and put yourself out there so that when opportunity meets up with your preparation, you find success.

Don't be afraid to admit you don't know to your students, your family, your colleagues, and yourself. Then spend the next chapter of your life trying to find out.

"Yes We Can!"

Now I'm not saying that we made it happen, I'm just saying that "Yes We Can!" was the motto for our America Sings! choral festival about a decade before there ever was a President Obama!

I'm just sayin'! I think he must have had a niece or nephew in a choir that went to an America Sings! festival in the Chicago area and went home with a very good slogan. I'm just sayin'!

"Yes We Can!" Or perhaps today you ought to focus on "Yes I Can!"

I have no doubt that an educated and experienced teacher such as yourself can take the steps necessary to reinvigorate your artistic life if you truly choose to do so. First you have to believe you can make the adjustments, believe that you are worthy of the people around you and their support, be confident enough to ask for help, forge ahead knowing you deserve this chance, and not be afraid simply because you don't know the precise outcome.

Positive thinking is not just a theory. It has been proved in test after test that people who think positively, even if at times the positivity seems manufactured, live happier and more productive lives. When a voice from someone else or the voice in your head says, "You don't have time to be teacher and artist," you respond, "Yes I can!" and proceed accordingly. When the same voices say, "But you haven't done your art for years!", the answer is, "Yes I can!" When money seems short, humiliation likely, ups and downs guaranteed, you know in your heart that art is something you need to do. You throw back your shoulders, build a stage in Soldier Field if necessary, and even if the only vote you get is your own, chant "Yes I can!"—and you will.

You are qualified.

I have said it before, but it bears repeating that music teachers, in fact teachers of most of the arts, are the most qualified people for their profession in the world. No other profession, except perhaps a professional baseball player whose parents played catch with him nonstop from the crib, started training so early and continued it as consistently as you. (Note to self, that professional baseball player's career is about over when yours is just getting started!)

You took lessons on piano or some other instrument from your earliest years and you never stopped practicing your art from that day on. Sure, there might have been times when your preparation was less intense than at other times, but by the time you started teaching in your chosen field you had literally decades of training. How many years does it take to become a brain surgeon or a rocket scientist? No offense to them, but you were way more qualified to begin your profession when you did than they were!

First you became qualified at a decent level to do your art. Then you took the training and spent the time and energy to become qualified to teach your art. Because of the discipline you learned early as an artist and the love you have for it, not to mention the training, the teaching came naturally to you and you are good at it.

Now you are profoundly qualified to handle both simultaneously. You are qualified to be both teacher and artist. There is no backtracking on those qualifications. You earned this chance.

Don't get tired.

One of my favorite three-word phrases: "Don't get tired." There's simply no time for it. I believe this to be true especially when it comes to teaching. This may be the one day you could have reached a particular student and you are too tired? I don't think so!

Don't you hate it when your fellow teachers stumble into the teachers lounge—or your students into the classroom—all whiny and moaning about how exhausted they are? I always think: "I'm tired! She's tired! He's tired! The whole world is tired; now keep it to yourself!"

I understand that there will be days when you feel less energetic than on others. Good health and energy are nothing to be taken lightly or for granted. But if lack of energy is a chronic problem that gets in the way of your teaching and/or artistic pursuits, maybe you need medical or psychological or spiritual counseling. If your schedule is just so jam-packed that you don't have time for rest, you can fix that. If you are tired because you are out of shape, you can fix that. If you are tired because the people around you are downers, you can fix that. If you are tired because of all of the demands your family, your administration, or you yourself are putting on you, you can fix that, too.

Remember the day you walked to school with your shoulders back and a spring in your step (okay, maybe it was first grade, but remember it). Today you have a choice. You can approach the day in a posture of exhaustion and despair or you can assume a posture of positive energy the way you did as a first-grader. I'm not suggesting that just because you pretend to have energy you suddenly will. But you will feel better than if you go around in a spent physical attitude. Works both ways.

Just walk faster.

I suppose it could have been simply "walk faster," but then it wouldn't have fit my theme of three little words.

This idea goes hand in hand with yesterday's admonition, "Don't get tired." The thing is, you rarely see depressed people walking fast! If you feel tired or depressed, pick up the tempo of your life. I mean literally "walk faster." Energy begets energy!

Jan Swenson, one of the great influences in my life as the supervising teacher of my student teaching experience, used to always say to me, "Life's too short to tiptoe through!" Maybe she said it only once, but it stuck like glue to me.

Plow boldly ahead (hmmm, three more good words), with confidence that your assertiveness and decisiveness will bear fruit.

Once you slow down it's hard to rev it up again. But, consciously, pick up the physical tempo of your life for a while and see if you don't reach your goals a lot faster.

What's your idea?

Eunice Kennedy Shriver was an impressive lady: sister to a president and two senators, founder of the Special Olympics. The breadth of her wake goes on and on.

One of things that impressed me the most was pointed out by her daughter, Maria Shriver, shortly after she died. Maria said that when she was a child, her mother would ask her and her brothers almost daily, "What is your idea?" Meaning, what do you plan to work on today or in this life that will make a difference? What do you plan to do with this opportunity called life?

From those who can do, much is expected.

So, artist/teacher, "what is your idea?" What thought or dream is needling in your heart and brain that you want to chase? Take a few moments to write down at least one clear idea of something you want to accomplish today, this month, this year, and then in this lifetime. It can be outrageous or at least outrageously ambitious. Today try not to think small and practical. Let your "idea" be as huge as your possibility, and your possibility is immense.

Every day from here on to eternity, make sure that, although your idea may morph, you always have one churning.

You are courageous.

You are courageous. We have already determined this by the very fact that you get up every day and put yourself in front of a classroom of students. A teacher of any subject and any age group displays an incredible amount of courage and confidence every single day.

Now your challenge is to use that courage to bring your life and life experiences into your work. In a way, teaching can be detached. Some are able to have their teaching life and then the rest of their life. But to be an artist is to bring all of you into your art. Every experience, every dream, every triumph, and every failure is brought to bear on your artistic output. This can be frightening. But you have the courage. Now show the will.

Ideas are free.

We have already discussed the fact that economic realities can hinder our pursuit of our art. We have to feed our families, pay the rent, heat the home, fill the gas tank. But it doesn't cost a thing to have an idea and go after it.

So much of the creation of art is in the mind. A writer spends a long time thinking about what to write before putting it in final form. One who draws has to doodle. One who composes has to tinkle (on the ivories, I mean!).

Today you are given permission to think about what you would like to say through your art if you were given a chance. It won't cost you a thing. Go ahead and doodle, ponder, dream, and...okay...tinkle.

Yesterday is history.

It doesn't matter if you are fourteen or 104: Yesterday is gone. There is nothing you can do about it. If you spend your time thinking about what could have been or maybe "used to be," you're wasting your opportunity to live now and in the future. It's okay to once in a while watch a video or listen to a recording of a concert or program of which you are particularly proud. But don't linger there too long or too often. Move on. Do something or create something new using that memory or past success to bolster your confidence to do something even better.

Sure, if you are a dancer you may not be able to leap as high. If you are a singer, you may not have the stamina you once had as a youth. Regardless, there are benefits to what age and maturity bring to the table. Your art will be different. You don't have to qualify it, better or worse; it's just different. You can't go back—it's over!

Even if you feel as if you're circling the drain, you've got time to produce. Yesterday was the springboard for what you are going to do today and tomorrow, and it's all good.

—12/9/13—

Art can heal.

I didn't just make this up. Studies over the course of many years have shown the healing nature of the arts. They also can bolster courage, which is why soldiers of yore marched to battle to the beat of the drums and dentists allow you to wear headsets and listen to your favorite rendition of "Drill, Ye Tarriers, Drill" as they do just that to your lower molars. The arts can bring comfort to the dying, which is why harpists, guitarists, and the like play such an important role in hospice care situations. Music especially can soothe crying babies (and their crying fathers), and on and on it goes.

Art can heal you, too. Look, it may not fix everything, but your involvement in this thing you love so much is what will help you find the courage to conquer your own trepidations. Despite any doubts you have about your future as an artist, focus on the art itself rather than others' opinions about your art or your pursuit of it. If you feel you lack confidence, focus on the art itself. If you are hurt by a bad experience in which your work was not what you'd hoped it would be, or even if your life is not now what you hoped it would be, focus on your art. It truly can heal.

Again, Vaughan Williams' *Fantasia on a Theme by Thomas Tallis.*

There, that ought to do it.

Art can heal. Just let it.

Never give up.

Or as Winston Churchill, an artist in his own right, said, "Never, ever give up."

Do you remember back on June 17th when I talked about this too-often-quoted quote? Well, someone recently pointed out to me the fact that this thought by good old Winston is often misquoted. What he precisely said was: "Never, never, in nothing great or small, large or petty, never give in except to convictions of honour and good sense. Never yield to force; never yield to the apparently overwhelming might of the enemy."

What he meant was, "Never, ever give up."

Why would you? How could you?

There will be difficult times ahead. There will be times when it will seem easier to retreat to the comfort of your classroom. (Did you ever think, when you first started teaching, that you would feel that the classroom was your refuge? But, it can be now, because you are experienced and good at it. Teaching, you know.)

Don't give up on your dreams of also being an artist. No, you might never feel as comfortable and safe doing your art as you do teaching. But, the act of art isn't necessarily supposed to be comfortable. Art is daring. So much about art cannot be known. It can be amorphous to say the least. It's difficult to do assessment on art! But art won't kill you either. You'll survive. The courage and tenacity you must muster to go after it may seem audacious to those around you and even to yourself. The changes you have to make in your life to pursue your art may seem daunting indeed. It might seem easier to ignore your artistic call. Don't.

Never give up. The world needs art—to heal it, inspire it, enlighten it, guide it, and, oh yeah, to teach it. The world needs your artistic contribution and so do you. Never give up. You won't on a student, so don't on yourself. Never give up. Never, ever give up.

Do your best.

How many times have you said that to a student who has doubts about his or her own potential? In the end, it's about all you can ask. But it's a tall order.

So "do your best" yourself, Teach!

That's all you can do, but it's the least you can do. We probably all had at least one person, a mentor of sorts, in our lives who somehow made us do better by ourselves. I had several. One of them was the first choreographer I worked under as a young singer/dancer wannabe. The other was the vocal coach for the same performing group. The choreographer's name was Tom Terrien and the vocal coach's name was Kurt Chalgren. They were genuine taskmasters. I name their names because they changed me forever and for good. They did not let me get away with doing pretty well. They demanded that I do my best. It wasn't always pleasant, but they made me do better. At least one time in each of our lives we need someone to kick our butts and say, "You can do better than that." If we're wise we listen to them and, guess what, we do better.

I encourage you to give this new artist/teacher approach to life your very best shot. It may go in different directions from what you think it will today. But the level of success you achieve will be a direct result of your honest and very best efforts. Do your best. No one could ask for more, but no one should expect any less from you, especially yourself.

Health is wealth.

I'm not what anyone would likely call a health nut. I have way too many vices that I'm not giving up to be classified as a health nut or health fanatic. But I do believe that when you have your health you have about everything. When you don't, it can be very difficult to carry through with any of the pithy three-word phrases we've explored so far.

I have one of those lower backs that occasionally take a hiatus. I mean, it doesn't take much. I can come down on my heel wrong, twist too quickly without warming up, or more often than not just sit too long at the computer. It hardly ever goes out when I'm dancing!

When it does "go out," nothing will make me feel older. You can age decades in an instant, and it's hard to think about anything other than just finding a comfortable position. You certainly aren't thinking about the development of the teacher/artist.

Take care of yourself. You know what it takes. Good food. Exercise. Well, there. That's about it. Good food and exercise.

Remember that nunnery we talked about, way back in January, where there are only three rules? Eat well. Sleep well. Laugh easily. I could be a nun there! I would love to be a nun there.

Eat well, sleep well, and laugh easily, and the rest of life's chase will take care of itself.

Be the change.

Mahatma Gandhi said, "We must be the change we wish to see in the world." You've probably seen this or a variation on bumper stickers or T-shirts. It's a brilliant thought.

As a teacher, you encourage this kind of behavior in your students. You expect them to look for examples of lives well-lived and emulate them. You encourage them to do something about it when they see injustice. You push them to "seize the day," or "go boldly where no man has gone before!" You admonish them not to just observe but to actively participate in the world they are inheriting.

You should do no less. You are the master of your own destiny, as far as human beings can control anything. So if you want something to change in your life, you have to be the one who initiates it and sees it through. What a great example you can be for your students, colleagues, family, and friends.

In a Gandhi-like thought, American writer Ramona L. Anderson is quoted as saying: "People spend a lifetime searching for happiness, looking for peace. They chase idle dreams, addictions, religions, even other people, hoping to fill the emptiness that plagues them. The irony is that the only place they ever needed to search was within."

In the end, like it or not, you can't not teach! It will probably be a big part of who you are. Now, by actively taking steps to change your own life in order to put more emphasis on your artistic interests, you once again teach the world how courageous teachers/artists/humans live. You make the change. It is not teach or do art. It is teach and do art.

Count your blessings.

I am sure there is truth to the thought that the happiest person is often he who is content with what he has. It is important to be grateful. Most of us teachers have pretty wonderful lives. We spend our time around other educated professionals. We work with young people who by their very nature keep us young and engaged with the fast-paced changes in the world. Most important, we have found the meaning in life in finding something meaningful to do with our lives. It ain't bad.

On the other hand, being grateful for the life we enjoy should not dissuade us from trying new things, having new dreams, and pursuing old ones. Just be joyful about it. You have a rewarding life already and now you are going to put some frosting on it.

I often talk about my approach to putting on a concert or program. Since I am a choral person I always try to put the emphasis on the music first. If it stinks, I try to fix that because I don't think you can cover up lousy music with all the costumes, lighting, and choreography in the world. But, if the music is already working for you, then each of these other elements that you add to this already successful "product" simply amplifies the success and takes it to another level.

You have a happy and rewarding professional life. Count it. Now all of the changes you make to it will enhance this already-successful time you spend on this great planet.

Dare to dream.

I think "Dare to dream" may have been a theme for one of the more recent Olympics. Or perhaps it was a Hallmark card. Either way, if it's good enough for Olympiads and Hallmark Cards it works for me.

It's okay to think that at whatever stage you are in your career, or for that matter in your life, you can still have dreams: dreams that you can pursue, dreams you deserve. Perhaps it doesn't take a lot of courage to dream. In fact it may not be something you can control. It is part of what it means to be human. (I don't know if other species have dreams. On occasion, I think I see and hear my dog Sadie chasing rabbits as she sleeps at my feet. But I don't know if her dreams have aspirations in the same way ours do, especially the dreams we have when we are awake.)

The courage comes in actively chasing after them. For me, I think it might be way more frightening to ignore your dreams than to pursue them. Ya got one shot. How scary to think you would ignore the very dreams and ideas that will make this one shot an extraordinary experience.

As artists we have the potential to live lives that are rewarding on an entirely different level than most. We just need the courage to get after that dream.

—— 2/3/13 ——

Dreams come true.

American artist Edward Hopper is credited with saying, "If you could say it with words there would be no reason to paint."

John Jacobson says, "If you could say it with words there would be no reason to sing."

Sometimes we need to exist on a different plane in order to find the truth, or the Truth, or what Picasso called "the lie." Art can take us there. As wild or unrealistic as our dreams may sometimes seem, art can take us there.

Dreams come true all the time and art will take us there.

—— ❧ ——

Make yourself useful.

There are so many choices one has to make in the world: choosing a school, a spouse, a career, a hair color...it just goes on and on. You made the choice to be a teacher, or perhaps at times it feels as if it chose you. You made a good choice. As I've said before, the meaning of life is to find something meaningful to do with your life, and you chose teaching. You have made yourself useful. Not everybody can say that.

Now, as you approach the next chapter and put a bit, or a lot, more emphasis on your artist self, there will more choices to make, as many as there are stars in the sky. As you make these choices, hopefully you will continue to make wise decisions that lead to an even more useful and meaningful life. In fact, the usefulness of the endeavor may continue to be your barometer as you make each small or grand adjustment to your already meaningful life. If you need a prayer or meditation to help, try this one that my lifelong friend—teacher and artist Mac Huff—and I penned together one dream-filled season.

The Ship I Sail

Lo, noble star among the heaven's lights,
Woe beyond my reach ne'er out of mortal sight,
Mine eyes are fast upon thy possibility.
Let this be the single star I see. Let this be the star I see.

O gallant voice quakes not in ocean's breeze,
Alas, nearly lost in quiv'ring human seas,
Calling men to honor and all to shy from fear.
Let this be the steady voice I hear. Let this be the voice I hear.

Ah ship of dreams, ah, ship of charity.
Sail forth in peace upon this wondrous sea.
Courage in your prow, in your wake, grace shall prevail.
Let this be the mighty ship I sail.
Let this be the voice, Let this be the star,
Let this be the ship I sail.

Do it now!

I actually had three three-word phrases in mind for today. One was "Just show up," sort of a take on Woody Allen's famous statement that much of life is really just about showing up. It's true. It certainly is true in teaching. There are days when you just have to be there, a beacon in the darkness of ignorance, a calming influence for students whose lives are full of turmoil, an anchor in the turbulent sea of life. Honestly, sometimes in teaching it hardly matters what you do, just that you are there to do it. Just show up. Good advice.

The other phrase I considered was "Seize the day!" "Carpe diem!" It's a dandy. Go rent the movie *Dead Poets Society* with Robin Williams and a bunch of other great actors. Then go back to school the next day and stand on your desk and recite "O Captain! My Captain!" Every other crazy thing you do will seem normal. I tear up just thinking about that movie.

But instead, I chose "Do it now!" Not nearly as poetic as "Carpe diem" or even as humorous as Woody Allen, but I think it is important that the changes you want to see in your life start immediately. Do one small thing that will move you in the direction of your artistic dreams. Clear out a creative space. Write a lyric or a melody. Sign up for a class. Go to a museum or a concert unlike any you've ever attended before. Do something proactive, not later, not tomorrow…now. Then show up and seize the rest of the day.

"Remember to live."

I put this three-word phrase in quotation marks because I first came across it reading the great German philosopher and teacher/artist Johann Wolfgang von Goethe. It's another of his enduring lessons.

As we go about our challenges and try to change our lives, it is important to live here, today, in the now. Wishing your life away will do only exactly that. Today is the day to revel in. You will still have dreams to ponder, events and experiences to look forward to, but it is so important to bask in the sunshine or the rain, wind, or hailstorm of this very moment. Right here. Right now! *"Gedenke zu leben!"* Remember to live!

"Knowledge is power."

English philosopher Sir Francis Bacon was one who said, "Knowledge is power." Said another way, "What you don't know could kill you." It was probably Archie Bunker or Bart Simpson who said that.

My father, the superintendent of schools, used to always tell us that teaching was the most secure profession in the world. "Just look at all the ignorance around you!" he would smilingly say.

The fact is, knowledge does make you powerful. Now as you try to make some adjustments in your life, the more you know about the consequences of those changes, the better. Perhaps this is a good time to go back to the divided piece of paper where you have listed the pros and cons of the changes you are about to make. (If you didn't do this on October 18th, here's another chance!) Or redraw it so that it is like one of those cause-and-effect tests we used to take: If I do this_____, this will happen_____. Put a plus sign before each positive effect and a minus sign in front of each negative.

For instance:

If I quit my church choir job, I will...

   –) Miss the money I earn.
   –) Miss the people I see every Wednesday night.
   –) Miss the spiritual feed that I get from my role there.
   +) Have Wednesday nights free to take that voice lesson.
   +) Be able to join the choir at the church my family actually attends.
   +) Have time to read the Sunday Times on Sundays.
   +) Never have to sing "Onward, Christian Soldiers" again.

Seriously, you can't foretell all of the consequences of your decisions, but writing them down and identifying the ones you are most concerned about may give you the power to make the changes most positive with the least collateral damage.

It is possible.

We are entering the season where the possible meets the Impossible. To me the Christmas season has always been a time in which we celebrate our human capacity to arrive at peace with the Impossible. We are capable of doing so.

It is also a good time of year to put things in perspective. The changes you are longing to make are totally doable. Why? Because you have done this before. You have been an active artist for most of your life and you're good at it. Granted, good is a relative term. But you were good enough to go to college, to master your art to the point that you became qualified to teach others to do it, and to act as an artist in an arts arena. All you're doing now is saying, "I want more of what I know I have in me." It's there. It never went away. You just desire to tap into it again as you did in your developing years.

Oh, it is possible. It may take a leap of faith. The same kind of leap of faith it took to realize that, although you can't comprehend the Great Thou Art, you can embrace It and be at peace with It here and now.

Be at peace now with the unknown factors of what you are going after. It is not impossible, and the Impossible will help you all along the way.

Got no strings.

When I was singing and dancing at Disney World, I did a puppet-style dance routine to the song "I've Got No Strings" from the movie *Pinocchio*. The props people would actually attach four elastic bands to me, one on each hand and one on each foot. The other ends of the bands were held by another dancer who played Geppetto, sitting on the shoulders of a third, tall dancer. Geppetto would pretend to work the "strings" as I danced in front of him like a puppet. (I can still do most of the routine, but my kicks get lower and lower each year.) Near the end of the song I would dramatically remove the strings from my feet and hands and dance freely about the stage, the puppet that became a real boy.

So for today's assignment I encourage you to think of four strings that are attached to you: strings that are causing you to behave in a certain way, strings that are not allowing you to move freely through your life as an artist. Label each of these strings either on paper or in your head. I am reluctant to suggest ideas for the strings, but maybe one would be something like, "I'm afraid I won't be as successful as an artist as I am as a teacher."

Now, before you get to remove this string, you need to design an action that will help you feel the strings loosen, or better yet disappear. Perhaps you could meditate on this idea: "Correct, I may not be as successful an artist as I am a teacher. But I can live with that because I teach others and I am doing this art for me. I will concentrate on being comfortable with the level of art I can achieve. Initially at least, I will be my only judge. I will be the only one to roll eyes, snicker, point, or critique my artistic efforts. I'm doing this for me." Then, think about one string loosening and the dance you are soon going to be able to do.

Believe in God.

It's Christmas Eve. Whether you are Christian or not, I believe that you need to believe in something greater than yourself. As an artist, your highest calling may be to illuminate not just the human condition, but also the human relationship to a Higher Authority.

Though the struggle to change your life may seem very lonely at times, you are not alone. First of all, look around at the remarkable people with whom you share this teaching profession. You have friends and colleagues who can help you along the way, just as you would help them in their life's journey.

And you are not alone, because the great Teacher/Artist who made you wants you to be the fully realized being of Her design. You were made to be an artist/teacher.

You might feel lonely. Loneliness happens. But you are not alone. Of all the nights of the year, perhaps this is the one when you just decide… to believe.

God is love.

My favorite of the three-word phrases. I believe this to be true. On Christmas Day it seems so obvious. Don't mess me up with a lot of details. That seems to be when we get ourselves in trouble. What is God? God is Love with a capital "L."

On Christmas Day the world seems full of Love.

Let the warmth of this Love help you conquer any nagging doubts you have about embracing the artist you want to be. It may not always be as obvious to feel as on a beautiful Christmas Day, but you are surrounded by the love of others who want the best for you. They love you and want you to pursue the dreams planted in you by the One called Love.

I love you.

Ooh! I'm in a loving mode! It happens 'round the holidays.

It's simple. Love is good. Hate is bad.

In all things.

So now, you are maybe sensing that conflict awaits as you make the moves to reconfigure the teacher/artist. There may be struggles for those who feel they deserve your attention and time. There may be financial stress. There may be confrontation when you have to say "no" to one so that you can say "yes" to yourself.

There are many ways to approach conflict, but none has proved more effective than love. Love and more love.

As each situation arises, I encourage you to address it with just such a remedy. The teacher/artists of the world need to embrace the role of showing others that this can be done. We have a lot of work to do. With the privilege of a life in the arts comes great responsibility. Teaching about love through our art may be the greatest of these.

And, by the way, I love you. Teachers who are also artists! What's not to love?

Love piles up.

The last of my three-word phrases about love. Love piles up. I love the image and idea that the more you love, the more love surrounds you. It piles up like leaves falling around you on a brisk autumn day.

Hope, too, piles up. That is why teaching is such a healthy profession. It is hard not to be hopeful around first-graders who are learning to read, write, and add things up. They look hopefully forward to new days and new ideas, loving every day.

It is hard not to be hopeful and full of love when you are around a fifth-grader who is excited and nervous about going into middle school, or an eighth-grader who can't wait for high school, or a freshman who wants to be anything but a freshman. How can you not be filled with hope when you know seniors and see how excited they are about getting out into the "real" world? If only they knew.

To be a teacher is to be surrounded by hope, love, and leaning forward. Now, let the hope and love in one part of your life bolster you in another. Keep loving others and yourself through this process of change. Keep your mind on the hopeful hearts of children. Be like them and let the love pile up around you.

Look for good.

It is easy to see all that is wrong with the world, and one should certainly go about with eyes wide open to injustice and hurt, grief and despair. But in every situation there is good as well, and we must be aware of it if we are going to help spread it around.

As you develop your art, look for the good in others and in yourself. You are good at so many things—teaching, for one, art for another. Every work of art need not be covered with pixie dust. In fact, art has often been the greatest form of exposé, showing the world the worst of ourselves in the hopes that we can do better by one another.

But as you get ready to take this flying leap into the abyss of an uncertain future, look around for the bright spots you can hang your hopes on. There you will find fellow teacher/artists to help you. There you will find positive inspiration for your own works. From goodness will come the courage. From goodness will come the confidence.

During this time of re-evaluation, dwell on the supportive people in your life. Think of all the resources at your disposal to help you achieve your dreams: friends, family, colleagues, libraries, museums, healthy food, classes, lessons, books, movies, art. All good stuff. Look for good.

You are valuable.

We don't tell people just how valuable they are. We need to practice it because we need to say it and they need to hear it.

I am particularly fond of public school teachers, mainly because I am a descendant of them, but also because a public school teacher doesn't have the luxury of teaching only the perfect kids—the ones with the perfect home, perfect teeth, and mother with the minivan. A public school teacher teaches whoever gets off the bus. Ain't it grand?

And because you take them all in, you are showing them through your example that each and every one of them is worth your effort. They deserve you.

By your dedication to them you are saying: "It doesn't matter if you're big or little, you're valuable. It doesn't matter if you're black or white, brown or pink, you're valuable. It doesn't matter if you're rich or poor, gay or straight, Christian or Jew, quick or slow, a soprano or a tenor, you are valuable."

Now on December 29th, as the year is winding down, dear teacher/artists, you need to be told that this is also true about you. The world needs you as a teacher and as an artist. Whatever it is that makes you you, we need it. All of it. That's why we're taking this journey together.

Fate is kind.

Some people don't believe this. I do. I believe that if you live a good life, a life filled with:

Yes we can ——— You are qualified ——— Don't get tired ——— Just walk faster ——— What's your idea? ——— You are courageous ——— I don't know ——— Ideas are free ——— Yesterday is history ——— Art can heal ——— Never give up ——— Do your best ——— Health is wealth ——— Be the change ——— Count your blessings ——— Dare to dream ——— Dreams come true ——— Make yourself useful ——— Do it now ——— Remember to live ——— Knowledge is power ——— It is possible ——— Got no strings ——— Believe in God ——— God is love ——— I love you ——— Love piles up ——— Look for good ——— and believing, knowing, trusting that you are valuable ——— Fate will ultimately treat you kindly.

It may not be this week, this month, or this year. It may not be until the day you meet your maker. Take a step, then the next and the next. And if your life's journey is honestly all of this, it will be okay. You, you teacher artist, are on the road to a kind fate of which you are so very worthy.

———

All is well.

I often have a very difficult time finishing the reading of a book. (Say nothing about writing one!) I get distracted. I get depressed. I worry that when this chapter is finished I have to go back to living in the world I've not had to dwell in as I read the book. Alas, here we are at the end of this book. Time to disengage from theory and get to the actual doing. Not so easy. Maybe even frightening. Go ahead. Close the book and begin. Put the book on a shelf, knowing you can return to it if you need a shot in the arm or give it to a friend who is trying to reintroduce artist self to teacher self. But you—you put it down. You have the courage. Now go out and be the artist you know you are. Be the artist and the teacher. This book is finished. You're getting started. Begin anywhere. But do begin. All over again. All is well, dear teacher, for there is an artist within you.

Acknowledgments

BE A STAR!
By John Jacobson and Roger Emerson
Copyright © 2011 by Hal Leonard Corporation

COME TO SHORE
By Audrey Snyder and John Jacobson
Copyright © 2006 by Hal Leonard Corporation

A NEW BEGINNING
By John Jacobson and Roger Emerson
Copyright © 2000 by Hal Leonard Corporation

THE SEA IS SO WIDE
By John Jacobson and Mac Huff
Copyright © 1991 by Hal Leonard Corporation

THE SHIP I SAIL
By John Jacobson and Mac Huff
Copyright © 2006 by Hal Leonard Corporation

SUPERSTAR
By John Jacobson and Mark Brymer
Copyright © 2012 by Hal Leonard Corporation

John Jacobson

Music Educator, Choreographer, Author

John Jacobson is internationally recognized for his large-scale music and choreography productions. His outstanding body of work includes producing hundreds shows in association with Walt Disney Productions (including the opening of Disney Tokyo), directing choreography for presidential inaugurations, and producing massive song and dance numbers for events such as NBC's Macy's Thanksgiving Day Parade.

His fans are legion, launching him as an internet sensation, through his entertaining and gleeful YouTube dance videos, which have an incredible track record for going viral, attracting millions upon millions of views.

With a bachelor's degree in Music Education from the University of Wisconsin-Madison and a Master's Degree in Liberal Studies from Georgetown University, John has written, composed, and choreographed musicals and choral works that have been performed by millions worldwide, as well as countless educational videos that have been incorporated into music teaching curriculums. John's works are published exclusively with Hal Leonard Corporation.

John is the founder and volunteer president of America Sings! Inc., a nonprofit organization that encourages young performers to use their time and talents for community service. John is also recognized internationally as a creative and motivating speaker for teachers and students involved in music education and was named a Presidential Point of Light by President Clinton. He founded the classroom standard *John Jacobson's Music Express* magazine (where he continues as Senior Contributing Writer), reaching nearly 4 million children world-wide.

John recently penned the new book *Double Dreams: Living a Life of Glee, Harmony, and Oh Yes....JAZZ HANDS!* and its DVD companion, *Double Dream Hands – Songs for Fun and Fitness.*

John's other works include jJump! DVD fitness series for kids (of all ages), his motivational book *A Place in the Choir,* and many new videos on his *Music Express* YouTube channel.